A TRUE CHRISTIAN IS: NOTW

A TRUE CHRISTIAN IS: NOTW

Jerry Hunter

New Harbor Press

RAPID CITY, SD

Copyright © 2019 by Jerry Hunter

All rights reserved. No part of this publication may be reproduced, distributed or transmitted in any form or by any means, without prior written permission.

Hunter/New Harbor Press
1601 Mt.Rushmore Rd, Ste 3288
Rapid City, SD 57701
www.newharborpress.com

A True Christian Is: NOTW/ Jerry Hunter. -- 1st ed.
ISBN 978-1-63357-170-9

Scripture quotations marked "ESV" are taken from The Holy Bible, English Standard Version. Copyright © 2000; 2001 by Crossway Bibles, a division of Good News Publishers. Used by permission. All rights reserved.

Scripture quotations marked (NLT) are taken from the Holy Bible, New Living Translation, copyright © 1996, 2004, 2007 by Tyndale House Foundation. Used by permission of Tyndale House Publishers, Inc., Carol Stream, IL 60188. All rights reserved.

CONTENTS

INTRODUCTION 1
CHAPTER 1: ACCEPTING CHRIST IN YOUR LIFE 7
CHAPTER 2: THE COMMANDS 27
CHAPTER 3: HELL 35
CHAPTER 4: FORSAKING THE TRUTH 39
CHAPTER 5: OUR CULTURE 63
CHAPTER 6: POLITICS, COURTS, AND ELECTIONS 85
CHAPTER 7: PROPHECY 101
EPILOGUE 119
ADDENDUM 127

INTRODUCTION

Revelation 3:20 (ESV)

Behold, I stand at the door and knock. If anyone hears my voice and opens the door, I will come in to him and eat with him, and he with me.

I am writing this book primarily to the generation called Millennials and those even younger. This generation has grown up in a culture that has turned their backs on God, or have never known God. They live in a culture that has been grossly silent and misinformed about our Lord.

Many have never read the Bible or do not believe in it. I want to show you just how import God's Word is and how reliable it is, and how it is truly the Word of the God that created you, and me, and this entire universe.

The Bible is a Divine Revelation. In the Bible we find out what God wants mankind to know about Himself and His plan.

The Bible is the only written revelation of God to man.

No one has ever successfully refuted the Bible. Many mock the Bible but avoid challenging it point by point. No one who has done in-depth research, honestly examining the evidence for the Bible's inspiration and truthfulness, has been able to disprove the Bible.

History records many who set out to disprove the Bible, who instead became believers.

Check out Josh McDowell and Lee Strobel two modern day men who set out in our times to disprove the Bible and are now ministers.

Our Bible is composed of 66 books, by about 40 different writers of various backgrounds, living during a period of about 1,600 years -- yet together they present one message. Such a miracle can only be explained by there being one divine Author who inspired of all these human writers. Jesus Christ is mentioned directly or indirectly in all 66 books.

The Bible writers came from many walks of life, including kings, peasants, philosophers, fishermen, herdsmen, poets, statesmen, scholars, soldiers, priests, prophets, a tax collector, a tent making rabbi, and a Gentile doctor.

The Bible was written in three different languages: Hebrew, Aramaic, and Greek.

The writings contained in the Bible belong to a great variety of literary types including history, law, poetry, educational discourses, parables, biography, personal correspondence, and prophecy.

Books written by men have no unity of thought on even one subject. Some of them invariably disagree with others. But there is perfect unity between the books of the Bible -- which speak of *hundreds* of subjects in many fields. There is no contradiction among them.

Who but God could produce such a book?

I pray this puts the Bible in the proper respective for you.

Some of you may be what the Bible calls "lukewarm" in your belief. Lukewarm Christians are not fully dedicated to Jesus Christ or serving your life for Him.

The book of Revelation can also be helpful to any person or Christian that God calls "lukewarm":

Revelation 3:16 (ESV)
16 *So, because you are lukewarm, and neither hot nor cold, I will spit you out of my mouth.*

There are numerous reasons why the younger generations have no religious affiliation or beliefs, and right now I want to focus on showing the importance of believing in our Savior Jesus Christ.

I will be straightforward in my writings because the subject matter is serious. Every person can receive the salvation of God if they open the door and let him in. But many people are driven by sin, and those sins are what I address in the book. God wants all people to be saved and He gives us time to repent of our sins.

1 Timothy 2:4 (ESV)
4 *who desires all people to be saved and to come to the knowledge of the truth.*

2 Peter 3:9 (ESV)
9 *The Lord is not slow to fulfill his promise as some count slowness, but is patient toward you, not wishing that any should perish, but that all should reach repentance.*

I am not a writer or a Bible scholar, but, I am a Christian. I have read and studied much over the last few years, and I realize how extremely important it is to know and follow our Lord and Savior Jesus Christ. And that is where I want to take you. I want to tell all who will listen why we are here on this earth, and how and why God wants us to live.

Let me tell you a little bit about me and why I want to spread these words I am writing. I wasn't born into a Christian home where I went to church each Sunday. But eventually my Dad did start taking me, my brother and sister to church. I'm not sure how old I was, maybe 10 or 11 or so. When we started we went when the doors were open, Sunday morning, Sunday evening and Wednesday nights. What I learned about being a Christian and my savior Jesus Christ was at church. There was no discussion on the Bible or devotions at my home. Only an occasional prayer at meals.

Probably the biggest influence on my Christian life at this point was the family of my Dad's brother. There was my aunt and uncle and five cousins — all boys. They were a devout Christian family, and a big influence on me. Two of those five boys became preachers of the Gospel of Christ.

One of the biggest failures in my life is that I did not raise my three children to come to know the Lord of our lives, Jesus Christ. He was never discussed in our home, other than an occasional prayer at meal time. There were no devotions or times that we discussed our Savior or the Bible. No direction in their lives on how they were to go. I consider this one of my biggest failures in my life. There were no directions from the parent such as Proverbs 22:6.

Proverbs 22:6 (ESV)
6 *Train up a child in the way he should go; even when he is old he will not depart from it.*

Because there was no commitment to Christ in my life in the year 2000 my marriage broke up. I was the reason, and I caused a lot of hurt to many people. My three children, all adults at the time, took this break up extremely hard. Relationships were strained, some still are, and they may never be healed.

But two years later, 2002, became a pivotal year in my life. I was alone and lonely. I had four good friends that encouraged me come to church with them, and I did. I was getting religious related emails, and I read them. I walked into a public restroom at work and found a religious handout. I picked it up, read it, and forwarded it on.

I came home from work one night past midnight and parked the car. A song came on the radio that I had never heard before. Instead of turning the radio off and going on inside I listened to the whole song. It was a song by Ricky Skaggs called Someone Is Praying for Me. Now, I had heard of Ricky Skaggs, but I knew nothing about any songs he sang, and the radio station I was listening to was not a country station. But I did get out of that car that night knowing that there was someone who was praying for me!

In 2002 cell phones were not as smart as they are now. In my work I always carried a small, pocket sized calendar. It was getting late in the year, and I was looking for one for 2003 everywhere I went. Finally I walked into a store and there was the calendars laying on the counter. I picked one up and guess what, at the top of the calendar it said:

> Smile Jesus Loves You and I Do Too.
> This is my commandment to you, love
> one another as I have loved you. John 15:12

On the back of the calendar were also four bible verses concerning Healing, Strength, and the Future.

Also along this time my daughter was encouraging me to read a book, or books, on the Left Behind series. I did read one or two and found them interesting, but I had a lot more to learn.

In October 2002 Billy Graham came to Texas Stadium in Irving, Texas. One of my four very good friends invited me to come along. Billy Graham was there for four nights. I went to three out of the four and worked the night I missed. After that crusade I went home and started praying. And then I was letting God back into my life, and He answered my prayers.

I prayed that God would bring me a woman that I could love and adore for the rest of my life, and God answered that prayer. I got remarried, and my wife and I started back to church and joined a Sunday School Class. The class we joined had a great teacher, and I was beginning to learn a lot about the Word of God. I read the Bible from Genesis to Revelation. I prayed to God and told Him that I wanted to learn as much about the Bible as I could before He called me home. This was another prayer that God answered. I am constantly in the Word now, and I am learning all that I can about the Bible and God's plan of salvation and the plan for our lives. Only since joining this Sunday School class have I really learned what it is to be a Christian!

I let Jesus in!

This is my reason for writing this book. I want to tell everyone I can what it really means to be a Christian, a True Christian, the way the Bible explains it.

CHAPTER 1

ACCEPTING CHRIST IN YOUR LIFE

1 Corinthians 10:31 (ESV)

So, whether you eat or drink, or whatever you do, do all to the glory of God.

The Purpose of Life
Have you ever asked yourself the question, "Why was I born?" Have you thought about how short a lifespan really is? Normal lifespans may reach to 80 or 90, sometimes longer. But how short is that time when you consider eternity? We were put on this earth to give glory to God, our maker and creator. What other reason could there be?

The Bible is clear about what God desires from Christians. God wants us to glorify His Son's name, Jesus Christ. He desires that we tell others about the "Good News" of the Gospel. That is what the Gospel is……Good News.

Consider these Bible verses:

Isaiah 43:7 (ESV)
everyone who is called by my name,

<u>whom I created for my glory</u>,
whom I formed and made."

2 Peter 3:18 (ESV)
But grow in the grace and knowledge of our Lord and Savior Jesus Christ. <u>To him be the glory</u> both now and to the day of eternity. Amen.

2 Corinthians 4:13-15 (ESV)
13 *Since we have the same spirit of faith according to what has been written, "I believed, and so I spoke," we also believe, and so we also speak,* **14** *knowing that he who raised the Lord Jesus will raise us also with Jesus and bring us with you into his presence.* **15** *For it is all for your sake, <u>so that as grace extends to more and more people it may increase thanksgiving, to the glory of God</u>.*

Habakkuk 2:14 (ESV)
14 *For the earth will be filled*
with the knowledge of <u>the glory of the Lord</u>
as the waters cover the sea.

My conclusion for the purpose of our short lives on this earth and how to give glory to Christ is this:

Every thought we have, every decision we make, every word we say, we should consider if this is in God's will. We should never do anything that is not in God's will.

This would include:
- The movies and television we watch.
- The attendance we give to our church.
- The person we marry.
- The manner in which we take care of our bodies.
- Our efforts to share God's Word with other.
- Our examples to others.

Anything! Anything! Every decision we make we should consult God for His approval.

Just remember that Jesus is right there with you! He knows your every thought and action. You can't hide it from Him.

The Bible is very clear as to what our purpose in life should be. Men in both the Old and New Testaments sought for and discovered life's purpose.

Solomon, the wisest man who ever lived, discovered the futility of life when it is lived only for this world. He gives these concluding remarks in the book of Ecclesiastes:

Ecclesiastes 12:13-14 (ESV)
13 The end of the matter; all has been heard. Fear God and keep his commandments, <u>for this is the whole duty of man</u>. 14 For God will bring every deed into judgment, with every secret thing, whether good or evil.

Solomon says that life is all about honoring God with our thoughts and lives and thus keeping His commandments, for one day we will stand before Him in judgment. Part of our purpose in life is to fear God and obey Him.

God desires at least three things for every Christian.
1. To know God's Word
2. To keep God's commands
3. To be a witness for Christ

TO KNOW GOD'S WORD

Our minds are renewed as we read the Bible. God transforms our thought patterns so they honor Him. God's Word holds countless layers of insight and meaning, it never grows stale. The more you grow in your relationship with Him, the more insights you will have into His character and how He operates.

TO KEEP GOD'S COMMANDS

Part of your destiny is to live in a righteous manner where God has placed you—and to do so consistently.

From looking at your life, people should be able to know what God considers right and wrong.

Apostle Paul describes the lives of the believers in Corinthians 2 Cor. 3:3:

2 Corinthians 3:3 (ESV)

3 *And you show that you are a letter from Christ delivered by us, written not with ink but with the Spirit of the living God, not on tablets of stone but on tablets of human hearts.*

Apostle Paul also addresses our example in Galatians.

Galatians 6:7-8 (ESV)

7 *Do not be deceived: God is not mocked, for whatever one sows, that will he also reap.* **8** *For the one who sows to his own flesh will from the flesh reap corruption, but the one who sows to the Spirit will from the Spirit reap eternal life.*

TO BE A WITNESS FOR CHRIST

Every Christian is called to an active ministry. That doesn't mean we will all be full-time preachers or missionaries. But with the guidance of the Holy Spirit, believers are to share the gospel through words and conduct.

God has a daily blueprint for your life that He is unfolding before you. Nobody else can fulfill your specific destiny. Trust the Holy Spirit to lead and empower you, and you will succeed in fulfilling the Lord's mission for your life.

Matthew 28:18-20 (ESV)

18 *And Jesus came and said to them, "All authority in heaven and on earth has been given to me. 19 Go therefore and make disciples of all* *nations, baptizing them in the name of the Father and of the Son and of the Holy Spirit, 20 teaching them to observe all that I have commanded you. And behold, I am with you always, to the end of the age."*

1 John 3:2 (ESV)
2 *Beloved, we are God's children now, and what we will be has not yet appeared; but we know that when he appears we shall be like him, because we shall see him as he is.*

God has an **eternal purpose** for each of us: to be saved and to become more like Christ. God's one overriding, eternal desire for you is that you trust Christ for your salvation and then mirror the attitudes, actions, and affections of His Son, Jesus Christ!

The Basics

John 3:16 (ESV)
16 *"For God so loved the world, that he gave his only Son, that whoever believes in him should not perish but have eternal life.*

John 14:6 (ESV)
6 *Jesus said to him, "I am the way, and the truth, and the life. No one comes to the Father except through me.*

Everyone, except maybe a few atheists, believe in eternity and Heaven. Why? Because God has placed that thought into our minds.

Ecclesiastes 3:11 (ESV)
11 *He has made everything beautiful in its time. Also, he has put eternity into man's heart, yet so that he cannot find out what God has done from the beginning to the end.*

Because God has placed this thought into our minds and all people want to spend eternity in Heaven rather that Hell many people cannot except that there is only one way to the one true God. So they conjure up other ways to suit their own beliefs.

But in reality there is one God, the one true God who made the Heavens and the Earth, and He made us. Much of the world today cannot accept that there is only one way to Heaven. Let's logically reason this out. If there are many ways to Heaven does that mean there are many gods. And if there are many gods or many ways to Heaven, are there many heavens? If there is only one true God isn't there only one true Heaven? And if there is only one true God and one true Heaven doesn't it make sense that God has left His Word here to us to tell us how to get to Heaven? The Bible is God's one true Word to us. If you read it and understand it you will see how it all fits together and is the one and only true way to live our lives while here on this earth and to eventually spend eternity with Him in the one true Heaven.

The Bible describes Christians as those who are forgiven of their sins and who have entered a personal relationship with Almighty God through faith in Jesus Christ.

Ephesians 2:8-9 (ESV)
8 *For by grace you have been saved through faith. And this is not your own doing; it is the gift of God, 9 not a result of works, so that no one may boast.*

Romans 10:9-10 (ESV)
9 *because, if you confess with your mouth that Jesus is Lord and believe in your heart that God raised him from the dead, you will be saved.* **10** *For with the heart one believes and is justified, and with the mouth one confesses and is saved.*

Now if you confess with your mouth that Jesus is Lord what all are you confessing to?

FAITH

Faith is a basic of Christian life. It is essential! The Bible defines faith in Hebrews 11:1:

Hebrews 11:1 (ESV)
1 *Now faith is the assurance of things hoped for, the conviction of things not seen.*

Also in Hebrews 11:6:

Hebrews 11:6 (ESV)
6 *And without faith it is impossible to please him, for whoever would draw near to God must believe that he exists and that he rewards those who seek him.*

Faith is the first basic confession that a Christian must make.

Romans 10:9 (ESV)
9 *because, if you confess with your mouth that Jesus is Lord and believe in your heart that God raised him from the dead, you will be saved.*

Faith grows when a person realizes they are totally lost. It is a conviction of sin. Each and everyone of us need to realize that we are lost sinners before we can realize that we need a Savior. When we accept Christ as that Savior we are willing to deny self and to suffer for the sake of Jesus Christ. True faith produces a humble and obedient heart. A true Christian's whole lifestyle, value system, speech, and attitude will surrender to Christ as Lord.

In Jesus' ministry He was not looking for large quantities of followers He was looking for "quality" followers. Jesus was looking, and still looking, for followers that believed in Him, that would devote their lives to Him, that would work to serve Him, that would be obedient to Him, and who would be willing to suffer and die for Him!

Jesus turned away many potential followers because they were not willing to yield their lives to Him. During His life on earth many only followed to see His miracles and get free food.

All Christians need to overcome the world that we are living in. If we are truly born of God, we will have a faith that cannot fail to overcome the world.

1 John 5:4 (ESV)
4 *For everyone who has been born of God overcomes the world. And this is the victory that has overcome the world—our faith.*

True faith is living the Christian life, not just talking about it.

Matthew 15:7-9 (ESV)
7 *You hypocrites! Well did Isaiah prophesy of you, when he said:* **8** *"'This people honors me with their lips, but their heart is far from me;* **9** *in vain do they worship me, teaching as doctrines the commandments of men.'"*

Jesus wants sincere dedicated followers who understand that following Him will not be easy. He addresses the issue of counting the cost of following Him in Luke 14:28-31:

Luke 14:28-31 (ESV)
28 *For which of you, desiring to build a tower, does not first sit down and count the cost, whether he has enough to complete it?* **29** *Otherwise, when he has laid a foundation and is not able to finish, all who see it begin to mock him,* **30** *saying, 'This man began to build and was not able to finish.'* **31** *Or what king, going out to encounter another king in war, will not sit down first and deliberate whether he is able with ten thousand to meet him who comes against him with twenty thousand?*

Jesus said that His followers will be hated for His name:

Matthew 10:22 (ESV)
22 and you will be hated by all for my name's sake. But the one who endures to the end will be saved.

The Apostle Peter had much to say in his writings about Christians suffering and being ready to suffer, being blessed for suffering, and learning from suffering. No other book in the Bible addresses the issue of Christian unjust suffering more than 1 Peter.

For example:

1 Peter 4:13-16 (ESV)
13 But rejoice insofar as you share Christ's sufferings, that you may also rejoice and be glad when his glory is revealed. 14 If you are insulted for the name of Christ, you are blessed, because the Spirit of glory and of God rests upon you. 15 But let none of you suffer as a murderer or a thief or an evildoer or as a meddler. 16 Yet if anyone suffers as a Christian, let him not be ashamed, but let him glorify God in that name.

The fiery trials we will endure purifies Christians and punishes those who do not obey the gospel. The suffering we do for Jesus, the denying self, carrying our cross all call for a wholehearted commitment to Him.

1 John 5:4 (ESV)
4 For everyone who has been born of God overcomes the world. And this is the victory that has overcome the world—our faith.

So "Faith" is the first thing we need. What follows?

In order to become a Christian, a person must fully accept as part of his or her own personal worldview the following core beliefs:

- **Jesus is the Son of God, and is equal with God**

Luke 22:70 (ESV)
70 *So they all said, "Are you the Son of God, then?" And he said to them, "You say that I am."*

Mark 3:11 (ESV)
11 *And whenever the unclean spirits saw him, they fell down before him and cried out, "You are the Son of God."*

- **Jesus was born of a virgin**

Matthew 1:18 (ESV)
18 *Now the birth of Jesus Christ took place in this way. When his mother Mary had been betrothed to Joseph, before they came together she was found to be with child from the Holy Spirit.*

- **Jesus lived a perfect, sinless life**

Hebrews 4:15 (ESV)
15 *For we do not have a high priest who is unable to sympathize with our weaknesses, but one who in every respect has been tempted as we are, yet without sin.*

John 8:29 (ESV)
29 *And he who sent me is with me. He has not left me alone, for I always do the things that are pleasing to him."*

Jesus was crucified to pay the penalty for our sins

Matthew 26:28 (ESV)
28 *for this is my blood of the covenant, which is poured out for many for the forgiveness of sins.*

1 Corinthians 15:2-4 (ESV)
2 *and by which you are being saved, if you hold fast to the word I preached to you—unless you believed in vain.* **3** *For I delivered to you as of first importance what I also received: that Christ died for our sins in accordance with the Scriptures,* **4** *that he was buried, that he was raised on the third day in accordance with the Scriptures,*

- <u>**Jesus rose from the dead**</u>

Luke 24:46 (ESV)
46 *and said to them, "Thus it is written, that the Christ should suffer and on the third day rise from the dead,*

Mark 16:6 (ESV)
6 *And he said to them, "Do not be alarmed. You seek Jesus of Nazareth, who was crucified. He has risen; he is not here. See the place where they laid him.*

- <u>**We are saved by the grace of God; that is, we cannot add to or take away from Christ's finished work on the cross as full payment for our sin**</u>

Ephesians 2:8-9 (ESV)
8 *For by grace you have been saved through faith. And this is not your own doing; it is the gift of God,* **9** *not a result of works, so that no one may boast.*

- <u>**All scripture is from God and without error.**</u>

2 Timothy 3:16 (ESV)
16 *All Scripture is breathed out by God and profitable for teaching, for reproof, for correction, and for training in righteousness,*

A person will not be saved without holding to the core beliefs.

After a person has come to believe the core beliefs they must repent of their sins and be "born again". Jesus explained this to a Pharisee named Nicodemus (one of the Jewish leaders) in the third chapter of John. Nicodemus came to Jesus at night (not to be seen by the other Pharisees) seeking to learn. Jesus told Nicodemus in the in the third verse that he must be "born again" to enter the kingdom of God.

John 3:3 English Standard Version (ESV)
3 *Jesus answered him, "Truly, truly, I say to you, unless one is born again he cannot see the kingdom of God."*

Apostle Peter also addresses being born again:

1 Peter 1:22-24 (ESV)
22 *Having purified your souls by your obedience to the truth for a sincere brotherly love, love one another earnestly from a pure heart,* **23** *since you have been born again, not of perishable seed but of imperishable, through the living and abiding word of God;*

Continuing in John, Nicodemus questions Jesus and His reply:

John 3:5-8 (ESV)
4 *Nicodemus said to him, "How can a man be born when he is old? Can he enter a second time into his mother's womb and be born?"* **5** *Jesus answered, "Truly, truly, I say to you, unless one is born of water and the Spirit, he cannot enter the kingdom of God.* **6** *That which is born of the flesh is flesh, and that which is born of the Spirit is spirit.* **7** *Do not marvel that I said to you, 'You must be born again.'* **8** *The wind blows where it wishes, and you hear its sound, but you do not know where it comes from or where it goes. So it is with everyone who is born of the Spirit."*

In verse 6 - it is saying the Holy Spirit gives birth to spiritual life.

Up to this point everything that Nicodemus had learned and worked for were worthless. All of his good works, extensive knowledge and great accomplishments were for nothing. Before Nicodemus was ready to hear the good news of Jesus' gospel he had to be emptied of his self confidence and accomplishments in order to see his need for a Savior. He had to start new with a new birth of the Holy Spirit if he hoped to be in the Kingdom of Heaven. The same is true with us. We are all born sinners. We need to see our need for a Savior, and we all start with a new birth of the Holy Spirit in order to see the Kingdom of Heaven.

The Holy Spirit does the work in transforming a sinner into a new creature.

2 Corinthians 5:17 (ESV)
17 *Therefore, if anyone is in Christ, he is a new creation. The old has passed away; behold, the new has come.*

After giving your life to Christ you will walk in a new direction. You will have a real purpose with the Holy Spirit living inside of you. Your former self was corrupt and deceitful. Your new self will be created after the likeness of God in true righteousness and holiness.

You will do away with your old self which is corrupt and deceitful. You will be renewed in the spirit of your minds. You will put on the new self created after the likeness of God in true righteousness and holiness (Ephesians 4:22-24).

Ephesians 4:22-24 (ESV)
22 *to put off your old self, which belongs to your former manner of life and is corrupt through deceitful desires,* **23** *and to be renewed in the spirit of your minds,* **24** *and to put on the new self, created after the likeness of God in true righteousness and holiness.*

And if you are truly born again you will begin to reflect Jesus to others. Our lives will change so that everyone who meets us can see Christ in us. And you will feel bad and remorseful when you sin.

The person who has believed will yearn to obey. The desire to do the will of God will be ever present in true believers

The true Christian that recognizes his sin and the grace of God are eager to share His word with everyone that does not know Him. Look at two examples in the Bible.

Jesus talked to the Samaritan woman at the well. He told her about the "Living Water" and what He also knew about her life. When she saw the truth of who Jesus was she returned to town and brought others back to see and hear Jesus. Her first impulse as a new believer was to go and tell others about Christ. When the people returned to see Jesus they asked Him to stay. Jesus did stay two more days and many were saved after hearing the Words of Jesus. (John 4:1-43).

The "Living Water" that Jesus gave the Samaritan woman was the Holy Spirit!

We see another example of Matthew, one of the Apostles. He was a crooked tax collector driven by greed. Jesus passed by Matthew sitting in the tax booth, and He told Matthew to follow Him. Matthew decided to have a banquet to introduce Jesus to his friends. Like most new believers, he wanted to bring everyone he knew to Christ.

The desire to proclaim one's faith is a common experience of new believers. In fact, some of the most zealous witnesses for Christ are brand-new believers.

A Transformed Life

Romans 12:1-2 (ESV)
1 *I appeal to you therefore, brothers, by the mercies of God, to present your bodies as a living sacrifice, holy and acceptable to God, which is your spiritual worship.* **2** *Do not be conformed to this world,*

but be transformed by the renewal of your mind, that by testing you may discern what is the will of God, what is good and acceptable and perfect.

Accepting Jesus Christ as your Lord and Savior and being "Born Again" is just the beginning of becoming a Christian. As I stated earlier in the section titled The Purpose of Life, a true Christian's life should be filled with serving and living for God. Every move, thought, or action should be taken with God's perspective in mind. **Following the will of God is for a lifetime.**

Romans 12:2 says to be transformed by the renewing of your mind. To start renewing your mind I suggest getting your Bible and start reading. Many pastors these days neglect study of the Old Testament and do not believe it is relevant in todays society. This is wrong. The Old Testament is extremely important and part of the entire process of knowing who Jesus is and why He came to earth. Additionally the Bible as a whole is 27% prophecy and this prophecy is in both the Old and the New Testaments. Much of it has already passed, but some of the most important prophecy is yet to come. And extremely important end times prophecy is very close. This is another reason I have undertaken writing this book, and we will get to this subject later.

When Adam and Eve were in the Garden of Eden, they sinned by eating the fruit of the forbidden tree and sin entered the world. Until this time there was no sin or death in the world. The penalty for Adam and Eve eating the fruit was death. Adam and Eve's sin resulted in everyone born on this earth is born a sinner.

Romans 5:12 (ESV)
12 *Therefore, just as sin came into the world through one man, and death through sin, and so death spread to all men because all sinned—*

Psalm 51:5 (ESV)
5 *Behold, I was brought forth in iniquity,* and in sin did my mother conceive me.

The Old Testament contains the Ten Commandments. The Commandments are rules to follow written by God. We are told in the Book of James that no man or women can enter Heaven if they violate just one of the commandments.

James 2:10 (ESV)
10 *For whoever keeps the whole law but fails in one point has become guilty of all of it.*

No one can keep the Ten Commandments. Apostle Paul tells us in Romans:

Romans 3:23 (ESV)
23 *for all have sinned and fall short of the glory of God,*

In Romans 12:1 Paul tells us that "by the mercies of God" we are to be "living sacrifices" to God. We become living sacrifices to God by not conforming to this world, but by being transformed by the renewal of our minds. A living sacrifice to God is one who does not conform, but is transformed. We are not to be conformed to this world. The unbelievers in this world walk in darkness. As believers we have been transferred to the Kingdom of Jesus Christ. Therefore, rather than continuing to live in darkness by conforming to this world, we are to be transformed by having our minds renewed.

The only way to replace the error of the world's way of thinking is to replace it with God's truth. Our transformation and renewing of our minds come from reading, hearing, and knowing the Word of God. We do this by faithful attendance each week in church, personal Bible study, and group Bible study. Doing this we learn that the Gospel is the "Good News" of Christ salvation and the purpose of His coming to this earth and dying for our sins.

REPENTANCE

When faith leads to Christ repentance must follow. If a person does not realize that they are sinners and need forgiveness they will not come to Christ. Repentance as Jesus characterized it involves a recognition of one's utter sinfulness and a turning from self and sin to God. Repentance is not a concept of change of heart. It is a total change of heart and direction. **It is a total conversion**.

When Nicodemus came to Jesus he was a leader of the Pharisees. He supposedly knew the law well and followed it. But Jesus told Nicodemus that he was basically ignorant of the law because he did not understand what it meant to be born again. This is the beginning of the gospel of Jesus. Salvation is impossible without a transforming rebirth according to the gospel of Jesus.

A repentant person turns to God, and away from evil. Their future is to serve God. Repentance is lifelong process of confession (1 John 1:9). The new Christian will reverse their formal lifestyle and begin to live for Christ.

1 John 1:9 (ESV)

9 *If we confess our sins, he is faithful and just to forgive us our sins and to cleanse us from all unrighteousness.*

The worse the sinner is, the more remarkable is his conversion.

Jesus spoke often about repentance: In Luke 13 in both verses 3 and 5 Jesus said,

"No, I tell you; but unless you repent, you will all likewise perish."

When Jesus first began His ministry he preached repentance:

Matthew 4:17 (ESV)

17 *From that time Jesus began to preach, saying, "Repent, for the kingdom of heaven is at hand."*

A genuine repentant person involves an aspect of remorse. It is a change of direction of the human will and a determined decision to forsake all sinfulness and pursue righteousness instead. A truly repentant person will be determined to abandon his disobedience and surrender to the will of Christ.

Where there is no noticeable difference in conduct, there can be no assurance that repentance has taken place (Matt. 3:8; cf. 1 John 2:3 – 6; 3:17).

Matthew 3:8 (ESV)
8 *Bear fruit in keeping with repentance.*

1 John 2:3-6 (ESV)
3 *And by this we know that we have come to know him, if we keep his commandments.* **4** *Whoever says "I know him" but does not keep his commandments is a liar, and the truth is not in him,* **5** *but whoever keeps his word, in him truly the love of God is perfected. By this we may know that we are in him:* **6** *whoever says he abides in him ought to walk in the same way in which he walked.*

1 John 3:17 (ESV)
17 *But if anyone has the world's goods and sees his brother in need, yet closes his heart against him, how does God's love abide in him?*

You will not repent of your sins until you realize that you are a guilty and disgraceful sinner in the presence of God, and that you deserve the wrath and punishment of God.

When you realize that you are bound for Hell only will you realize you need to repent of your sins. Then you will take up your cross and follow Jesus.

Repentance is a complete surrender of will and an inevitable change of behavior — a new way of life, not just a different opinion, and a continual way of your old life. Apostle Paul summed it up very well in 2 Timothy 2:12:

2 Timothy 2:12 (ESV)
if we endure, we will also reign with him; if we deny him, he also will deny us;

CHAPTER 2

THE COMMANDS

John 14:15 (ESV)
15 "If you love me, you will keep my commandments

After we accept Jesus Christ as our Lord and Savior we are to live our lives for Him. Everything we do is for Him and to bring glory to Him. We are to follow His commands.

In the words of Jesus:

John 15:14 (ESV)
14 You are my friends if you do what I command you.

If you Google "How do you follow the commands of Jesus" you will certainly get numerous articles addressing this subject. One site even listed 300 commands of Jesus. All of the commands I saw were biblical and they say we should live our lives — as Jesus did.

As covered in the last chapter one of the commands of Jesus is Repentance.

Matthew 4:17 (ESV)
17 From that time Jesus began to preach, saying, "Repent, for the kingdom of heaven is at hand.

Being repentant from your sins is a requirement to become a Christian, but that is not a one time commitment. Repentance is a constant necessity because as imperfect Christians we will sin each day. Therefore, we must recognize our sins, repent of them daily, and strive not to commitment those sins.

And of course one of the commands is to love your enemies.

Matthew 5:44-46 (ESV)
44 *But I say to you, Love your enemies and pray for those who persecute you,*

This can be a hard one, but it is a commandment of Jesus. Let's all work on it.

Jesus gave us what we call the Golden Rule:

Matthew 7:12 (ESV)
12 *"So whatever you wish that others would do to you, do also to them, for this is the Law and the Prophets.*

And Jesus tells us to make disciples:

Matthew 28:18-20 (ESV)
18 *And Jesus came and said to them, "All authority in heaven and on earth has been given to me.* **19** *Go therefore and make disciples of all nations, baptizing them in the name of the Father and of the Son and of the Holy Spirit,* **20** *teaching them to observe all that I have commanded you. And behold, I am with you always, to the end of the age."*

Notice carefully how Christ approaches this subject and how He says what He does. First He said that "all authority" has been given to Him. Secondly He says "Go" and make disciples. Jesus gave a command. He did not say, "Will you go?", "Can you go?", or "You can go." Jesus gave a command to all of His followers to go and make disciples.

If I have talked to you about following Christ and giving your life to Him this is why. One thing is Jesus commands it. Another thing is that when you accept Christ and understand Christ you want the whole world to know what a wonderful life that He offers. And you want to keep as many people as you can from going to Hell.

But one of the most important things that Jesus said was this:

Luke 9:23 (ESV)
23 And he said to all, "If anyone would come after me, let him deny himself and take up his cross daily and follow me.

This is a key command of Jesus for Christians to follow Him. In the day that Jesus was crucified the Romans required convicted criminals to carry their own crosses to the place of crucifixion. Jesus' command to "take up your cross and follow Him" was a command to be willing to die in order to follow Him. **This is dying to self. It is a total surrender of your life to follow Him.**

And, of course, this has happened. Many Christians have given up theirs lives to follow Christ. Many have died for Him, but their reward in Heaven will be great. Following Jesus is easy when life is going well. But, our true commitment to Jesus is determined during difficult times and struggles. And Jesus did tell His followers that trials would come.

Jesus assured us that trials will come to His followers (John 16:33).

John 16:33 (ESV)
33 I have said these things to you, that in me you may have peace. In the world you will have tribulation. But take heart; I have overcome the world."

Discipleship demands sacrifice, and Jesus never hid that cost.

Jesus never said that it would be easy to follow Him. When people came to Him and seemingly wanted to follow Him, He questioned them to determine their commitment. In many commitment was lacking because they were unable to face the cost of following Him. They were not willing to take up their cross.

Any true believer in Jesus Christ must be willing to count the cost of following Him. Christians are constantly under attack in our culture today. The Word of God is being attacked. Believers are called bigots because they believe what God has told us in the Bible. Crosses are being attacked that were built many years ago. A marine was kicked out of the military because she refused to take a Bible verse off of her computer. People are being attacked for having an open Bible laying on their desk. Stories come up like this every day. And you will be attacked.

Jesus was not, is not, looking for a large quantity of followers. He is looking for a quality of followers. People whose commitment to Him is true and loyal and dedicated.

In counting the cost of following Jesus a Christian should consider these questions:

- Are you willing to follow Jesus if it means losing some of your closest friends?
- Are you willing to follow Jesus if it means alienation from your family?
- Are you willing to follow Jesus if it means the loss of your reputation?
- Are you willing to follow Jesus if it means losing your job?
- Are you willing to follow Jesus if it means losing your life?

Commitment to Christ means taking up your cross daily, giving up your hopes, dreams, possessions, even your very life if need be for the cause of Christ.

Only if you willingly take up your cross may you be called His disciple:

Luke 14:27 (ESV)

27 *Whoever does not bear his own cross and come after me cannot be my disciple.*

The reward is worth the price.
What does Jesus mean when He says follow me?

Mark 8:34 (ESV)
34 *And calling the crowd to him with his disciples, he said to them, "If anyone would come after me, let him deny himself and take up his cross and follow me.*

John 12:24-26 (ESV)
24 *Truly, truly, I say to you, unless a grain of wheat falls into the earth and dies, it remains alone; but if it dies, it bears much fruit.* **25** *Whoever loves his life loses it, and whoever hates his life in this world will keep it for eternal life.* **26** *If anyone serves me, he must follow me; and where I am, there will my servant be also. If anyone serves me, the Father will honor him.*

Jesus says following Him results in:
   Works of Righteousness
   A Heart That Responds To The Reality of Christ's Lordship
   Steadfast obedience to His commands

The Bible tells us that we cannot earn our way to Heaven, but it also tells us that if you are a true follower of Jesus you will respond with Works of Righteousness.

Ephesians 2:8-9 (ESV)
8 *For by grace you have been saved through faith. And this is not your own doing; it is the gift of God,* **9** *not a result of works, so that no one may boast.*

James 2:17 (ESV)
17 *So also faith by itself, if it does not have works, is dead.*

Famed English Pastor Charles Spurgeon said this about works:

"Although we are sure that men are not saved for the sake of their works, yet we are equally sure that no man will be saved without them."

True faith is manifest only in obedience.

A heart that responds to the reality of Christ's Lordship will never again fall into the cold, hard-hearted, determined unbelief and rebellion of our former state.

Steadfast obedience to His commands is necessary and expected. It is the result of genuine love for for Jesus Christ.

Jesus' offer was of eternal life and forgiveness for repentant sinners, but at the same time it was a rebuke to outwardly religious people whose lives were devoid of true righteousness.

Jesus talked about salvation and following Him. But He also taught about those who failed to take His Words seriously. Jesus taught that there was a narrow gate leading into Heaven, and few would find it. He taught that there would be false prophets and false teachers, and that we must recognize them. Jesus also taught that some who thought they were correctly following Him would hear these words on judgment day:

Depart from me, I never knew you!

Matthew 7:13-23 (ESV)

13 *"Enter by the narrow gate. For the gate is wide and the way is easy that leads to destruction, and those who enter by it are many.* **14** *For the gate is narrow and the way is hard that leads to life, and those who find it are few.*

15 *"Beware of false prophets, who come to you in sheep's clothing but inwardly are ravenous wolves.* **16** *You will recognize them by their fruits. Are grapes gathered from thornbushes, or figs from thistles?* **17** *So, every healthy tree bears good fruit, but the diseased tree bears bad fruit.* **18** *A healthy tree cannot bear bad fruit, nor can a diseased tree bear good fruit.* **19** *Every tree that does not bear good*

fruit is cut down and thrown into the fire. **20** *Thus you will recognize them by their fruits.*
21 *"Not everyone who says to me, 'Lord, Lord,' will enter the kingdom of heaven, but the one who does the will of my Father who is in heaven.* **22** *On that day many will say to me, 'Lord, Lord, did we not prophesy in your name, and cast out demons in your name, and do many mighty works in your name?'* **23** *And then will I declare to them, 'I never knew you; depart from me, you workers of lawlessness.'*

A true Christian must be willing to forsake all for Him (Luke 14:33) — that is, nothing takes precedence over Christ. And the true believer will desire to do whatever He commands.

Luke 14:33 (ESV)
33 *So therefore, any one of you who does not renounce all that he has cannot be my disciple.*

The mark of a true disciple is not that he never sins, but rather that when he does sin he inevitably returns to the Lord to receive cleansing and forgiveness. This is the reason that God called King David a man after His own heart.

A true Christian's faith is neither fragile nor temporary. It is a dynamic and ever-growing commitment to the Savior.

Let me leave this chapter with one final warning.

Jesus said that we would be hated for His name. Many Christians have been martyred for their faith in Christ and their refusal to deny Him. In our current day and time more Christians are being martyred than in the total number up until this time. Let me remind you, a true Christian will not and cannot deny Christ.

Matthew 10:33 (ESV)

33 *but whoever denies me before men, I also will deny before my Father who is in heaven.*

Some may say the Apostle Peter denied Christ. Yes he did. But at this time Jesus had not risen from the grave. The apostles did not fully understand the plan of salvation until after Jesus arose. Later in Peter's ministry he did give his life for Jesus Christ. Secular history said that he was martyred on a cross upside down, because he did not feel worthy to die in the same manner as Jesus.

Following Christ is truly dying to self and living for Jesus!

CHAPTER 3

HELL

Revelation 21:8 (ESV)
8 But as for the cowardly, the faithless, the detestable, as for murderers, the sexually immoral, sorcerers, idolaters, and all liars, their portion will be in the lake that burns with fire and sulfur, which is the second death."

Hell is real folks. God created Hell for Satan and his fallen angels that rebelled against Him. Those living on this earth are subject to the same discipline if we fail to accept God's forgiveness and grace. God does not want anyone to go to Hell, and He gives us ample opportunity to come to Him and repent of our sins.

2 Peter 3:9 (ESV)
9 The Lord is not slow to fulfill his promise as some count slowness, but is patient toward you, not wishing that any should perish, but that all should reach repentance.

Do you know that Jesus spoke more on Hell than He did Heaven? Look at what Jesus says about Hell in the Gospel of Mark.

Mark 9:43-48 (ESV)

43 *And if your hand causes you to sin, cut it off. It is better for you to enter life crippled than with two hands to go to hell, to the unquenchable fire.* **45** *And if your foot causes you to sin, cut it off. It is better for you to enter life lame than with two feet to be thrown into hell.* **47** *And if your eye causes you to sin, tear it out. It is better for you to enter the kingdom of God with one eye than with two eyes to be thrown into hell, 48 'where their worm does not die and the fire is not quenched.'*

He says in verse 43 — the fire is unquenchable. And is verse 48 He again says the fire in unquenched but He also mentions that the worms do not die.

In Matthew 13 twice Jesus refers to Hell as the fiery furnace and place of darkness where there will be weeping and gnashing of teeth (v. 42 and 50).

Read closely the parable that Jesus gave in Luke:16:19-31:

19 *"There was a rich man who was clothed in purple and fine linen and who feasted sumptuously every day.* **20** *And at his gate was laid a poor man named Lazarus, covered with sores,* **21** *who desired to be fed with what fell from the rich man's table. Moreover, even the dogs came and licked his sores.* **22** *The poor man died and was carried by the angels to Abraham's side. The rich man also died and was buried,* **23** *and in Hades, being in torment, he lifted up his eyes and saw Abraham far off and Lazarus at his side.* **24** *And he called out, 'Father Abraham, have mercy on me, and send Lazarus to dip the end of his finger in water and cool my tongue, for I am in anguish in this flame.'* **25** *But Abraham said, 'Child, remember that you in your lifetime received your good things, and Lazarus in like manner bad things; but now he is comforted here, and you are in anguish.* **26** *And besides all this, between us and you a great chasm has been fixed, in order that those who would pass from here to you may not be able, and none may cross from there to us.'* **27** *And he said, 'Then I beg you, father,* *to send him to my father's house—* **28** *for I have five brothers—so that he may warn them, lest they also come into this place of torment.'* **29** *But Abraham said, 'They have Moses and the Prophets; let them hear them.'* **30** *And he said, 'No, father Abraham, but if someone goes to them from the dead, they will repent.'* **31** *He said to him, 'If they do not hear Moses and the Prophets, neither will they be convinced if someone should rise from the dead.'"*

Now, look and think about this: the rich man's state of being when in Hell. His senses and personality were fully engaged. He had his sight, his speech, his hearing, he had taste, he had feeling, and he had his memory.

Now think about spending forever, and forever, and forever in an unquenchable fire and darkness. Remembering your rejection of Jesus. Remembering those who tried to tell you about Jesus and the importance of making Him the primary facet of your life. Wanting just a touch of water. And hearing all of the screams of the people with you in pain.

There is a popular Christian song called "I Can Only Imagine". It is a Christian view of Heaven and meeting Jesus. How will it be, how will we react. Now imagine this. Imagine being in Hell. Imagine being there forever, and forever, and forever with no hope!

Now here is where everyone should be concerned. Bad people will go to Hell. But, some good people will go to Hell also! People can be good, caring, and loving people. They may be good to the homeless, protect animals, contribute to worthy charities. They may do many good things. But here is the key — we are saved by the Grace of God. You cannot earn your way to Heaven.

Ephesians 2:8-10 (ESV)
8 *For by grace you have been saved through faith. And this is not your own doing; it is the gift of God,* **9** *not a result of works, so that no one may boast.* **10** *For we are his workmanship, created in Christ Jesus*

for good works, which God prepared beforehand, that we should walk in them.

You cannot be saved by works so that you may boast about it in Heaven. You have to accept Jesus Christ as your Lord and Savior, and then when you walk in the footsteps of Jesus you will work for Him — spreading His Word, serving the church, and helping widows and orphans etc.

James 2:24-26 (ESV)
24 *You see that a person is justified by works and not by faith alone.* **25** *And in the same way was not also Rahab the prostitute justified by works when she received the messengers and sent them out by another way?* **26** *For as the body apart from the spirit is dead, so also faith apart from works is dead.*

Rahab believed, and Rahab worked to help the Jewish spies, and Rahab was saved.
All of us will have eternal life. It will be either in Heaven or in Hell. Christians preparing for Heaven begins right here while we are living on this earth! Our entire lives on this earth are to be lived for Him, 100% of the time.

1 Corinthians 10:31 (ESV)
So, whether you eat or drink, or whatever you do, do all to the glory of God.

Salvation is not just about avoiding Hell; it's about accepting true life in Jesus Christ.

CHAPTER 4

FORSAKING THE TRUTH

Postmodernism

Matthew 24:11 (ESV)
And many false prophets will arise and lead many astray.

Postmodernism is a philosophy that is becoming a part of the church today.

Postmodernism is a philosophy that says absolute truth does not exist. Those who believe in this philosophy deny long held beliefs, and they maintain that all viewpoints are valid.

Postmodernism leads to relativism. Relativism …. is the idea that views are relative to differences in perception and consideration. There is no universal, objective truth according to relativism; rather each point of view has its own truth.

Postmodernism and relativism views have led to the "*Emerging Church*". The emerging church is "supposedly" a Christian movement of the late 20th and early 21st centuries. These churches are called by a number of different names but they are far different than traditional Christian churches.

With the combination of these three philosophies you come up with a church that believes all truth is relative. That means what is right for one group is not necessarily right or true for everyone. The most obvious example of this is sexual morality. Christianity teaches that sex outside of marriage is wrong. Postmodernism say this may apply to Christians, but it is not truth for those who are not Christians. This view has led to sexual immorality becoming extremely permissive in our society.

Postmodernism argues that what society says is illegal, such as drug use or stealing, is not necessarily wrong for the individual.

Postmodernism's rejection of absolute truth leads many people to reject the Bible.

Since they reject the Bible they reject that Christ is the only way to Heaven. Christians are ridiculed as arrogant, intolerant, and bigoted by those who believe there are many paths to Heaven.

Postmodernist are told that if they invite Jesus into their hearts, accept Him as personal Savior, or believe the facts of the gospel, that is all there is to it. The aftermath is appalling failure, as seen in the lives of millions who have professed faith in Christ with no consequent impact on their behavior. Who knows how many people are deluded into believing they are saved when they are not?

Recognition of personal sin is a necessary element in understanding the truth of salvation. Salvation is for people who hate their sin and want to turn away from the sins of this life. It is for individuals who understand that they have lived in rebellion against a holy God. It is for those who want to turn their life around, to live for God's glory.

Christians believe God is the source of absolute truth. In fact, Jesus Christ proclaimed himself to be the Truth in John 14:6:

John 14:6 (ESV)
6 *Jesus said to him, "I am the way, and the truth, and the life. No one comes to the Father except through me.*

In postmodernism, all religion, including Christianity, is reduced to the level of opinion. Christianity asserts that it is unique and that it does matter what we believe. Christians say sin exists, sin has consequences, and anyone ignoring those truths has to face those consequences.

Christians cannot afford to be apathetic about the truth God has put in our trust. It is our duty to guard, proclaim, and pass that truth on to the next generation.

1 Timothy 6:20-21 (ESV)
20 *O Timothy, guard the deposit entrusted to you. Avoid the irreverent babble and contradictions of what is falsely called "knowledge,"* **21** *for by professing it some have swerved from the faith. Grace be with you.*

Many popular books written by leading figures in the *"Emerging Church"* are filled with a flood of vulgarity and worldliness onto Christian booksellers' shelves. Obscenity is one of the main trademarks of the Emerging style. Most authors in the movement make extravagant use of filthy language, and sexual innuendo. They often indicate an approval for ungodly aspects of secular culture. They believe what makes a postmodern ministry so easy to embrace is that it doesn't demonize our culture. Postmodern devotees aren't challenged to reject the outside world like traditional Christian fundamentalist beliefs. The differences between secular culture and Christianity is a big purpose for me writing this book.

The Bible tells us in numerous places about apostasy and false teachers coming into the church. We are warned to on our guard, to be alert, and to know God's Word.

Jeremiah 17:5 (ESV)
Thus says the Lord: "Cursed is the man who trusts in man and makes flesh his strength, whose heart turns away from the Lord.

2 Timothy 4:3 (ESV)
For the time is coming when people will not endure sound teaching, but having itching ears they will accumulate for themselves teachers to suit their own passions,

Vying for the faith has never been easy. But the postmodern shift has made the challenge much more difficult than ever.

In order for us to avoid being sucked into the Emerging Church movement or any apostasy teaching we must know the Word of God.

The Bible steadily tells us that it is every Christian's duty to study and interpret Scripture correctly.

Proverbs 2:1-5 (ESV)
1 *My son, if you receive my words and treasure up my commandments with you,* **2** *making your ear attentive to wisdom and inclining your heart to understanding;* **3** *yes, if you call out for insight and raise your voice for understanding,* **4** *if you seek it like silver and search for it as for hidden treasures,* **5** *then you will understand the fear of the Lord and find the knowledge of God.*

Psalm 119:9 (ESV)
9 How can a young man keep his way pure? By guarding it according to your word.

2 Timothy 2:15 (ESV)
15 *Do your best to present yourself to God as one approved, a worker who has no need to be ashamed, rightly handling the word of truth.*

Christianity has always affirmed the accuracy of Scripture. That means we believe God has spoken distinctly in His Word. The postmodernized idea that everything should be up for discussion and nothing is ever really sure or settled is a plain and simple denial of the accuracy of Scripture. Anyone who cites religious beliefs as a reason to reject another person's way of life is automatically viewed with the same contempt that used to be used to describe religious heretics. **The culture around us has declared war on all biblical standards.**

Paul writes in **Romans 12:2: ESV**
Do not be conformed to this world, but be transformed by the renewal of your mind, that by testing you may discern what is the will of God, what is good and acceptable and perfect.

Don't be conformed to postmodernism; don't be conformed to modernism. In fact, don't be conformed to any worldly "ism," but rather, follow God's Word listed above: "be transformed by the renewal of your mind, that by testing you may discern what is the will of God, what is good and acceptable and perfect".

Muslims

John 14:6 (ESV)
Jesus said to him, "I am the way, and the truth, and the life. No one comes to the Father except through me.

MUSLIMS

My highlight verse says no one comes to the Father except through Him. This excludes Muslims, Buddhist, Hindus, or any other religion that doesn't believe this statement from Jesus. Only those who follow Jesus Christ will enter Heaven.

In this section I will focus primarily on Muslims. Islam is the second largest religion in the world next to Christianity. Our country has a focus on the Muslims that astounds me today. They will get a pass when a Christian will get accused. This again is because the world will hate Christians because they hate Christ.

But let's look at the primary differences in Christians and Muslims because the differences are incompatible. The founders of these two religions: Jesus and Muhammed. Muhammed lived in the 600's AD. He claimed to be the last prophet and said he received a revelation from an angel of God. He initially feared his revelation had come from Satan. I believe that his revelation actually did come from Satan. Satan is the deceiver, and he started with Eve in the garden. And God tells us in 2 Corinthians 11:14:

2 Corinthians 11:14 (ESV)
14 And no wonder, for even Satan disguises himself as an angel of light.

1 John 4:1 (ESV)
4 Beloved, do not believe every spirit, but test the spirits to see whether they are from God, for many false prophets have gone out into the world.

The teachings of Muhammed:

<u>He sanctioned the beating of wives.</u>

The listed scripture below is from the Qur'an, the Muslim scripture.

(Sura 4:34)
Men are the protectors and maintainers of women, as Allah has given some of them an advantage over others, and because they spend out of their wealth. The good women are obedient, guarding what Allah would have them guard. As for those from whom you fear disloyalty, admonish them, and abandon them in their beds, <u>then strike them</u>. But if they obey you, seek no way against them. Allah is Sublime, Great.

<u>He sanctioned spreading his religion by force.</u>

(Sura 9:5)
When the Sacred Months have passed, <u>kill the polytheists wherever you find them</u>. And capture them, and besiege them, and lie in wait for them at every ambush. But if they repent, and perform the prayers,

and pay the alms, then let them go their way. Allah is Most Forgiving, Most Merciful.

He believed in executing unbelievers by cutting their throats.

(Sura 47:4)
When you encounter those who disbelieve, <u>strike at their necks. Then, when you have routed them, bind them firmly</u>. Then, either release them by grace, or by ransom, until war lays down its burdens. Had Allah willed, He could have defeated them Himself, but He thus tests some of you by means of others. <u>As for those who are killed in the way of Allah, He will not let their deeds go to waste</u>.

He taught that Allah does not love sinners.
   (Surah 3:140)
If a wound afflicts you, a similar wound has afflicted the others. Such days We alternate between the people, that Allah may know those who believe, and take martyrs from among you. <u>Allah does not love the evildoers</u>.

Islam teaches that the day of judgment will involve a person's good and bad deeds being weighed in a balance—so the standard for judgment is one's own actions.

(Surah 7:8-9)
7. *We will narrate to them with knowledge, for We were never absent.* **8.** *The scales on that Day will be just. Those whose weights are heavy-it is they who are the successful.*

(Surah 21:47)
We will set up the scales of justice for the Day of Resurrection, so that no soul will suffer the least injustice. And even if it be the weight of a mustard-seed, We will bring it up. Sufficient are We as Reckoners.

The Qur'an denies the death of Jesus on the cross (Surah 4:157–158). If you will be saved, you must save yourself.

(Surah 4:157–158)
157. And for their saying, "We have killed the Messiah, Jesus, the son of Mary, the Messenger of Allah." In fact, they did not kill him, nor did they crucify him, but it appeared to them as if they did. Indeed, those who differ about him are in doubt about it. They have no knowledge of it, except the following of assumptions. Certainly, they did not kill him. **158**. *Rather, Allah raised him up to Himself. Allah is Mighty and Wise.*

Differences in Islam and Christianity

To really understand the differences in Islam and Christianity you must look at the countries in the Middle East that are predominately Muslim populations. One recent example is of a lady by the name of Asia Bibi in Pakistan, a predominately Muslim country that protected Osama Bin Laden.

Asia Bibi

In Pakistan in 2009 Asia Bibi, a Roman Catholic, was arrested after a dispute with Muslim colleagues, who accused her of tainting a cup of water by drinking from it as a Christian. The prosecution against Bibi alleged that she responded to abuse from her colleagues by insulting Islam's Muhammad, a crime carrying the death penalty in Pakistan. She was found guilty and sentenced to hanging in 2010.

Asia was on death row until October 2018 when Pakistan's Supreme Court acquitted Bibi, asserting the witnesses who testified to her blasphemy had lied and, by using Islam to defame others, had committed their own crime of blasphemy.

In response to the ruling, thousands of Islamists, most of the radical Tehreek-e-Labaik Pakistan Party (TLP), took to the streets of Islamabad and other major cities demanding her death and the death of the three judges who freed her.

Experts on religious persecution agreed that, in this climate, Asia Bibi's life remains in imminent danger. They said that Asia Bibi is not safe in Pakistan, nor her family ... nor any of the Christians in Pakistan (or those brave Supreme Court Justices) at this point!"

Asia, her husband, and their children should definitely leave the country, and the U.S. should offer asylum. This is the perfect example of who should get asylum! An extremely credible fear of persecution, since the Islamist jihadists have sworn to kill her.

[At this writing Asia Bibi has not yet been rescued from Pakistan]

Meriam Ibrahim

In May 2014 in Sudan a court sentenced a pregnant, Christian Sudanese woman to death by hanging after she refused to renounce her faith, a decision Amnesty International called "abhorrent."

Meriam Ibrahim, 27, was convicted on charges of "apostasy" — the crime of abandoning or renouncing a religion. The court also ordered Ibrahim — who married a Christian man in 2011 and is eight months pregnant — to receive 100 lashes for "adultery" because her marriage is considered void under sharia law. The couple has a child, a 20-month-old boy, who was in detention with her.

Court officials gave Ibrahim three days to recant Christianity and return to Islam. When the deadline expired, Ibrahim told religious clerics in court in the capital of Khartoum, "I am Christian." Amnesty International says Ibrahim was raised as an Orthodox Christian, her mother's religion, because her Muslim father was absent during much of her childhood.

Meriam eventually did give birth while still in shackles inside her squalid prison, and reported on the heartbreak, angst and pride of her husband as she faced her ordeal behind bars.

The embassies of the United States, United Kingdom, Canada and the Netherlands in Khartoum released a statement expressing deep concern over the ruling, and Meriam was eventually released.

Sudan's penal code criminalizes the conversion of Muslims to other religions, which is punishable by death. Muslim women in Sudan are further prohibited from marrying non-Muslims, although Muslim men are permitted to marry outside their faith. Children, by law, must follow their father's religion.

Comparing the teachings of Muhammed with Christ we find:

<u>**Jesus Christ was above reproach in every way.**</u>

2 Corinthians 5:21 (ESV)
For our sake he made him to be sin who knew no sin, so that in him we might become the righteousness of God.

<u>**The commandment of Jesus was:**</u>

John 13:34 (ESV)
A new commandment I give to you, that you love one another: just as I have loved you, you also are to love one another.

<u>**And Jesus' plea was this:**</u>

Luke 23:34 (ESV)
34 *And Jesus said, "Father, forgive them, for they know not what they do." And they cast lots to divide his garments.*

<u>**God's standard for judgment is absolute perfection—the righteousness of Christ. No one can on this earth can meet that standard.**</u>

Romans 3:23 (ESV)
23 *for all have sinned and fall short of the glory of God,*

<u>**But God in His grace and mercy has given His Son as the substitute for our sin:**</u>

Colossians 2:13 (ESV)
13 *And you, who were dead in your trespasses and the uncircumcision of your flesh, God made alive together with him, having forgiven us all our trespasses,*

We cannot save ourselves, so we turn to Christ, our sinless Savior and the author and finisher of our faith.

Hebrews 12:2 (ESV)
2 *looking to Jesus, the founder and perfecter of our faith, who for the joy that was set before him endured the cross, despising the shame, and is seated at the right hand of the throne of God.*

The Differences

Christians and Muslims do not have the same understanding of who God is. Because of essential differences between the Christian and Muslim concepts of God, the two faiths cannot both be true. The God of our Bible solves the problem of sin by giving His Son.

Faithful Muslims are faced with a terrible choice: obey the violent commands of an omnipotent deity whose mercy is given only to the most passionate and devoted followers, or give themselves up as hopelessly lost and headed for punishment.

Christians should not regard Muslims with hatred, but instead with compassion and love. Because their eyes are blinded to the truth:

2 Corinthians 4:4 (ESV)
4 *In their case the god of this world has blinded the minds of the unbelievers, to keep them from seeing the light of the gospel of the glory of Christ, who is the image of God.*

We should pray for Muslims and ask God to show them the truth, revealing His promise of mercy and freedom in Christ:

2 Timothy 2:24-26 (ESV)
24 *And the Lord's servant must not be quarrelsome but kind to everyone, able to teach, patiently enduring evil,* **25** *correcting his opponents with gentleness. God may perhaps grant them repentance leading to a knowledge of the truth,* **26** *and they may come to their senses and escape from the snare of the devil, after being captured by him to do his will.*

In fact God is revealing His truth to them in todays day and time. Many Muslims are having dreams of Jesus and coming to Christ. Let's keep praying for them.

Tradition & The Scriptures

Matthew 15:6 (ESV)
6 *' So for the sake of your tradition you have made void the word of God.*

In the verse quoted above Jesus was speaking to the Pharisees. Jesus identified the Pharisees for who they were....hypocrites. Jesus told His listeners to respect the scribes and Pharisees due to their position of authority but not to follow in their footsteps because they did not practice what they preached. The Pharisees only wanted to be seen. They followed their "traditions" not the Word of God.

I touched on this subject in the section on Postmodernism, but I want to look into another area where the church is mislead. There are several verses in the Bible about not adding to or taking away from the scripture. The Bible is all we need to follow God's Words and commands. The Bible is same today as it was yesterday, and will be tomorrow.

Matthew 23:3-5 (ESV)
3 *so do and observe whatever they tell you, but not the works they do. For they preach, but do not practice.* **4** *They tie up heavy burdens,*

hard to bear, and lay them on people's shoulders, but they themselves are not willing to move them with their finger. **5** *They do all their deeds to be seen by others. For they make their phylacteries broad and their fringes long,*

The Pharisees religion was only for show because their hearts "had not been transformed". Jesus' words may have seemed crude, but there was so much at stake that the Pharisees did not follow. Those who followed the Pharisees and scribes were being kept from following God because their teaching contradicted God's Word. Jesus addresses at least one of the reasons their teaching was a contradiction in Matthew 15.

Matthew 15 (ESV) Traditions and Commandments
1 *Then Pharisees and scribes came to Jesus from Jerusalem and said,* **2** *"Why do your disciples break the tradition of the elders? For they do not wash their hands when they eat."* **3** *He answered them, "And why do you break the commandment of God* **for the sake of your tradition?** **4** *For God commanded, 'Honor your father and your mother,' and, 'Whoever reviles father or mother must surely die.'* **5** *But you say, 'If anyone tells his father or his mother, "What you would have gained from me is given to God,"* **6** *he need not honor his father.'* **So for the sake of your tradition you have made void the word of God.** **7** *You hypocrites! Well did Isaiah prophesy of you, when he said:*
   8
   "'This people honors me with their lips,
   but their heart is far from me;
   9
   in vain do they worship me,
   teaching as doctrines the commandments of men.'"

Here Jesus is talking about honoring your father and mother, but this principle applies to all of the entirety of the Word of God. Jesus spoke firmly against the deception of Satan out of a desire for people to know truth and find life in Him and not be mislead by tradition or teaching as doctrines the commandments of man. (In verses 8 and 9 Jesus is quoting from Isaiah 29:13).

The Pharisees were giving equal, or greater, authority to oral tradition, saying the traditions went all the way back to Moses. Evolving over the centuries, the Pharisaic traditions had the effect of adding to God's Word, which is forbidden:

Deuteronomy 4:2 (ESV)
2 *You shall not add to the word that I command you, nor take from it, that you may keep the commandments of the Lord your God that I command you.*

There are other verses about adding to or taking away from God's Word.

Deuteronomy 12:32 (ESV)
32 *"Everything that I command you, you shall be careful to do. You shall not add to it or take from it.*

Revelation 22:18-19 (ESV)
18 *I warn everyone who hears the words of the prophecy of this book: if anyone adds to them, God will add to him the plagues described in this book,* **19** *and if anyone takes away from the words of the book of this prophecy, God will take away his share in the tree of life and in the holy city, which are described in this book.*

And in Second Timothy God tells us this:

2 Timothy 3:16 (ESV)
16 *All Scripture is breathed out by God and profitable for teaching, for reproof, for correction, and for training in righteousness,*

Like the Pharisees, many people today participate in religious practices because of human tradition and command rather than Divine command. Some churches openly bind religious requirements on the basis of "tradition." They have elaborate rituals and technical rules, like the Pharisees, but they do not base them on Scripture. Instead, they justify them on the grounds of tradition.

Other denominations follow other forms of human laws: decrees of councils, pronouncements of human church officers, or official creeds written by leaders. They appeal to these as their authority for doctrine and practice. These human authorities, like the Pharisees' commands, sometimes bind what God has not bound and sometimes release people from things God has bound.

So once again, Jesus never rebuked the Pharisees or anyone else for teaching that people need to carefully and respectfully obey Divine law. What He did rebuke people for was binding human traditions or following human commands that differ from God's law. Surely, we too need to take care to make sure we are not guilty of being mislead by tradition.

God's Word is absolutely sufficient in itself.

Psalm 119:160 (ESV)
160 *The sum of your word is truth, and every one of your righteous rules endures forever.*

2 Timothy 3:15-16 (ESV)
15 *and how from childhood you have been acquainted with the sacred writings, which are able to make you wise for salvation through faith in Christ Jesus.* **16** *All Scripture is breathed out by God and profitable for teaching, for reproof, for correction, and for training in righteousness,*

2 Peter 1:20-21 (ESV)

20 *knowing this first of all, that no prophecy of Scripture comes from someone's own interpretation.* **21** *For no prophecy was ever produced by the will of man, but men spoke from God as they were carried along by the Holy Spirit.*

God's declaration in Scripture is that it, and it alone, is this final authority in all matters of faith and morals.

"The Scriptures cannot be altered" is a clear statement of the truth of the Bible. If we accept Christ as Lord, we also must accept his testimony to the Bible as God's Word.

Thus, there is only one written source from God, and there is only one basis of truth for the Lord's people in the Church.

The Word of the Lord says as a commandment in Proverbs 30:5-6:

Proverbs 30:5-6 (ESV)
5 *Every word of God proves true; he is a shield to those who take refuge in him.* **6** *Do not add to his words, lest he rebuke you and you be found a liar.*

God commands that we are not to add to His Word: this command shows emphatically that **it is God's Word alone that is pure and uncontaminated.**

How is scripture to be accurately interpreted?

The term "sola Scriptura" or "the Bible alone" is a short phrase that represents the simple truth that there is only one special revelation from God that man possesses today, the written Scriptures or the Bible. Scripture states this concept repeatedly and emphatically. The very phrase "It is written" means exclusively transcribed, and not hearsay. The command to believe what is written means to believe only the pure word of God. What is at stake before the All Holy God is His incorruptible truth.

The principle of "sola Scriptura" is basic to accurate interpretation of Scripture. Psalm 36:9 explains:

Psalm 36:9 (ESV)
9 For with you is the fountain of life; in your light do we see light.

The Apostle Paul said the same thing in his first letter to the Corinthians.

1 Corinthians 2:13 (ESV)
13 And we impart this in words not taught by human wisdom but taught by the Spirit, interpreting spiritual truths to those who are spiritual.

The Apostle Peter, under the inspiration of the Holy Spirit, declares, "knowing this first, that no prophecy of Scripture is of any private interpretation. For prophecy came not by the will of man: but holy men of God spoke as they were moved by the Holy Ghost" (**2 Peter 1:20-21**). Logically then, **Peter makes it very clear that in order to maintain the purity of Holy God's written word, the source of interpretation must be from the same pure source as the origin of the Scripture itself.**

Scripture can only be understood correctly in the light of Scripture, since it alone is uncorrupted. It is only with the Holy Spirit's light that Scripture can be comprehended correctly. The Holy Spirit causes those who are the Lord's to understand Scripture.

John 14:16-17 (ESV)
16 And I will ask the Father, and he will give you another Helper, to be with you forever, 17 even the Spirit of truth, whom the world cannot receive, because it neither sees him nor knows him. You know him, for he dwells with you and will be in you.

John 14:26 (ESV)

26 *But the Helper, the Holy Spirit, whom the Father will send in my name, he will teach you all things and bring to your remembrance all that I have said to you.*

Since the Spirit does this by Scripture, obviously, it is in accord with the principle that Scripture itself is the infallible rule of interpretation of its own truth "it is the Spirit that beareth witness, because the Spirit is truth" (I John 5:6).

1 John 5:6 (ESV) Testimony Concerning the Son of God
6 *This is he who came by water and blood—Jesus Christ; not by the water only but by the water and the blood. And the Spirit is the one who testifies, because the Spirit is the truth.*

If you want to be true to God in this important matter, follow His instruction:

Proverbs 1:23 (ESV)
23 *If you turn at my reproof, behold, I will pour out my spirit to you; I will make my words known to you.*

For final truth and authority, all that we need is the Scripture. Scripture is the authoritative record that Holy God has given His people. We do not have a single sentence that is authoritatively from the Lord, outside of what is in the written word.

The Bible is our only book to guide us, teach us, and lead us to Him and on to Heaven. The Bible was written for all times — for ancient history, for today, and for the future. Look closely at your church. Is your church following tradition or the Word of God? Are there things in their tradition that are not in the Bible? The Bible is our only source of knowledge for us to follow. Don't be mislead. Follow only what is in God's Word.

Discernment

Hebrews 5:14 (ESV)
14 But solid food is for the mature, for those who have their powers of discernment trained by constant practice to distinguish good from evil.

As the writer of Hebrews says living our lives for Christ takes discernment in determining good from evil. In the three illustrations I have provided, Postmodernism, Muslims, and Tradition it takes discernment to see the misleading teachings of these groups. It will take discernment to distinguish any false teaching from the true teaching of Jesus Christ.

Discernment is the ability to decide between truth and error, right and wrong. It is the process of making careful distinctions in our thinking about truth. But true discernment runs deeper than just knowing the different between truth and error. True discernment means not only distinguishing the right from the wrong; it means distinguishing the primary from the secondary, the essential from the indifferent, and the permanent from the transient. And, yes, it means distinguishing between the good and the better, and even between the better and the best. True discernment will lead to the ability to think biblically about all areas of life. It is necessary for the Christian to take hold of the discernment that God has provided for in His precious truth!

Expounding on the highlight verse at the top of the page the writer of Hebrews lays out the need for discernment.

Hebrews 5:11-14 (ESV)
11 About this we have much to say, and it is hard to explain, since you have become dull of hearing. 12 For though by this time you ought to be teachers, you need someone to teach you again the basic principles of the oracles of God. You need milk, not solid food, 13 for everyone who lives on milk is unskilled in the word of righteousness, since he is a child. 14 But solid food is for the mature, for those who

have their powers of discernment trained by constant practice to distinguish good from evil.

The writer here is expressing how very important it is to learn the scriptures of God. He stresses the need to become a "mature" Christian to gain the discernment to determine the good from the evil. Christians are not to just sit around and say they are a Christian. We are to continue to learn and improve our knowledge of the Word of God. Knowing the Word is the only way to avoid the apostasy and false teachings that are going on in the world.

Discernment is something we need to ask for and seek if we truly desire to live righteously.

Hosea 14:9 (ESV)
Whoever is wise, let him understand these things;
whoever is discerning, let him know them;
for the ways of the Lord are right,
and the upright walk in them,
but transgressors stumble in them.

As Christians we need to ask for and seek discernment. We understand the reasons for seeking and knowing discernment from the scriptures below:

1 Thessalonians 5:21-22 (ESV)
21 *but test everything; hold fast what is good. 22 Abstain from every form of evil.*

1 John 4:1 (ESV)
4 *Beloved, do not believe every spirit, but test the spirits to see whether they are from God, for many false prophets have gone out into the world.*

These verses tell us to hold on to what is good, abstain from evil, and do not believe every spirit because of the many false prophets (and teachers) in the world! We are responsible as Christians to know the truth and to follow it. Discernment is necessary.

So, how does one increase spiritual discernment? First, recognize that God is the only one who can increase wisdom, pray for it (James 1:5; Philippians 1:9).

James 1:5 (ESV)
5 If any of you lacks wisdom, let him ask God, who gives generously to all without reproach, and it will be given him.

Philippians 1:9 (ESV)
9 And it is my prayer that your love may abound more and more, with knowledge and all discernment,

Then, knowing the wisdom to distinguish good from evil comes by training and practice, go to the Bible to learn the truth and, by meditation on the Word, reinforce the truth.

Paul goes on to say in Philippians 1 the benefits of discernment:

Philippians 1:10-11 (ESV)
10 so that you may approve what is excellent, and so be pure and blameless for the day of Christ, 11 filled with the fruit of righteousness that comes through Jesus Christ, to the glory and praise of God.

Discernment is of crucial importance to our lives as believers in Christ, and with it comes great benefits. Proverbs 3:21–24 says:

Proverbs 3:21-24 (NLT)
21 My child, don't lose sight of common sense and discernment. Hang on to them,
22 for they will refresh your soul. They are like jewels on a necklace.

23 *They keep you safe on your way, and your feet will not stumble.*
24 *You can go to bed without fear; you will lie down and sleep soundly.*

The Bible makes it clear that discernment is something that we should all desire and that it is necessary to help us to grow in our faith and keep us from being deceived (Hebrews 5:14).

The key to living an uncompromising life lies in one's ability to exercise discernment in every area of his or her life. Failure to distinguish between truth and error leaves the Christian subject to all manner of false teaching. False teaching then leads to an unbiblical mindset, which results in unfruitful and disobedient living—a certain recipe for compromise.

God's Word provides us with the needed discernment about every issue of life.

It is written in the Book of 2 Peter 1:3:

2 Peter 1:3 (ESV)
3 *His divine power has granted to us all things that pertain to life and godliness, through the knowledge of him who called us to his own glory and excellence,*

It is through the "true knowledge of Him," that we have been given everything we need to live a Christian life in this fallen world. We have true knowledge of God through the pages of His Word, the Bible!

Peter goes on to say that such knowledge comes through God's granting "to us His precious and magnificent promises" (2 Peter 1:4).

2 Peter 1:4 (ESV)
4 *by which he has granted to us his precious and very great promises, so that through them you may become partakers of the divine nature, having escaped from the corruption that is in the world because of sinful desire.*

This is what Christians must do to develop spiritual discernment. We must know the Word of God so well that, when the false teaching appears, we can recognize it. By knowing and obeying the Word of God, we will be trained to constantly distinguish good from evil. We will know God's character and will. This is the heart of spiritual discernment – being able to distinguish the voice of the world from the voice of God, to have a sense that "this is right" or "this is wrong." Spiritual discernment fends off temptation and allows us to "hate what is evil; cling to what is good" (Romans 12:9).

Romans 12:9 (ESV) Marks of the True Christian
9 *Let love be genuine. Abhor what is evil; hold fast to what is good.*

CHAPTER 5

OUR CULTURE

John 17:16 (ESV)
16 They are not of the world, just as I am not of the world.

LIVING IN OUR CULTURE

Are you a true Christian! Or do you just call yourself a Christian and not truly follow Christ. Does your family identify as Christians and may claim to follow Jesus, but they do not. A true Christian is one who has received Jesus Christ as their personal Lord and Savior.

John 1:12 (ESV)
12 But to all who did receive him, who believed in his name, he gave the right to become children of God,

One who is not a true Christian will deny the inspiration of Scripture and the necessity of repentance. They disregard Hell and obedience to Christ. They celebrate and tolerate sin such as abortion and homosexual marriage. They have no devotion to Jesus and deny that He is the only way to Heaven.

One who simply identifies as a Christian find themselves a church that follows the preceding characteristics..

One of the biggest deterrents to living a Christian life is the culture in which we live. The culture is diametrically opposed to the Christian life. Satan is the god of this world, the one we live in. Satan wants his world filled with sin. It is morally bankrupt. The problem lies with the Christian in deciding what activities in our culture should a Christian participate in. The Christian must be strong to avoid the temptation of living in Satan's culture. The Christian must be strong to live the life that God desires.

In Ephesians 4:29 Paul addresses the speech of a Christian:

Ephesians 4:29 (ESV)
29 *Let no corrupting talk come out of your mouths, but only such as is good for building up, as fits the occasion, that it may give grace to those who hear.*

The New Living Bible Translations (NLT) puts it this way: "Don't use foul or abusive language".

Professing Christians are always watched by others to see if we are actually following our faith. Our lifestyle should be lived as Christ would expect — above reproach. Wherever we go or what ever we do we should always be cognizant of the appearance we have with others, and we should also realize that God is watching us and knows our every move or thought. The greatest single cause of atheism in the world today is Christians who acknowledge Jesus with their lips, walk out the door, and deny Him by their lifestyle.

We live in this world, but we are not separated from it. We go to the same stores and interact with society's non-Christians. In John 17:16 Jesus prays for the Christians living in this world. He states:

John 17:16 (ESV)
16 *They are not of the world, just as I am not of the world.*

Christians do not belong to this world. We are no longer conformed to the values and ways of living in the culture and society around us. We belong to the kingdom of God and, therefore, have a new identity and loyalty to the King and his Kingdom. Therefore, while we are in the world, we do not belong to or embrace the world as those who do not belong to Jesus Christ.

The Christians in the world are hated by the world! Below is a verse of Jesus praying to God on how He gave the world the Word of God, but the world hates the followers of Jesus.

John 17:14 (ESV)
14 *I have given them your word, and the world has hated them because they are not of the world, just as I am not of the world.*

Because we do not conform to the world culture we are mocked, ridiculed, detested, and hated for our counter-cultural ways of Christianity. Jesus told His followers that they would be hated because He was hated. Being in the world and not of the world causes Christians to be hated by the world who does not accept the King in whose Kingdom we gladly live.

We are told in Romans 12:2

Romans 12:2 (ESV)
2 *Do not be conformed to this world, but be transformed by the renewal of your mind, that by testing you may discern what is the will of God, what is good and acceptable and perfect.*

1 John 5:19 (ESV)
19 *We know that we are from God, and the whole world lies in the power of the evil one.*

Christians live in this world despite the hatred and contempt of the society, our culture. Christians do not compromise or conform to the world due to this hatred because that would deny our identity of a Christ follower. Nor, do we retaliate with violence or force.

Christians are to respond like Jesus and suffer the hatred, mocking, and contempt as we glorify God in our trials.

By remaining in the world, we love those who hate us, bless those who curse us, and give our lives away for those who have not given their lives to Jesus Christ.

John 17:15 (ESV)
15 *I do not ask that you take them out of the world, but that you keep them from the evil one.*

To accept Jesus Christ as your Savior you need to count the cost of being a Christian.

Are we willing to embrace this suffering? Can a Christian just sit home and wait for Christ return? Yes, we need to count the cost, no we can't just sit home and wait. We are to be a witness for Christ. We don't shy away from the evil forces of hatred. We move forward with love and compassion.

John 17:18 (ESV)
18 *As you sent me into the world, so I have sent them into the world.*

We live in a society that is perverse, ungodly, and full of sin, and we must be different because God commands it. He commands us to be like himself—separate, holy, and righteous.

Every Christian needs to know who they are, what they are called to do, and why we live in this particular way in the world. **If your life is not different from the world remember that God delivered you from worldliness so you could know him and live for him!**

The depravity of the Gentile world was due to its willful ignorance of God. The world has hardened its heart against God and so is alienated from him intellectually and in every other way. The world is ignorant of God, but Christians have come to know him. The secular mind is hostile to Christ's teaching, but the believer joyfully and continually **makes progress** in learning all about Christ.

True believers **desire** the Word of God, and God's righteousness. Jesus says:

Matthew 4:4 (ESV)
4 But he answered, "It is written,
"'Man shall not live by bread alone,
but by every word that comes from the mouth of God.'"

We desire God's Word and the righteousness that comes from obeying it. Christ says:

Matthew 5:6 (ESV)
6 *"Blessed are those who hunger and thirst for righteousness, for they shall be satisfied.*

True believers desire to see people saved, discipled, and daily conforming to God's image. They have a new self—a new nature from God.

CULTURE'S ACTIVITIES OPPOSED TO GOD

ABORTION

Dr. Barnard Nathanson was one of the pioneers in wanting legalized abortion. Dr. Nathanson worked in New York where abortion was legal before the Supreme Court decision on Roe v. Wade was handed down. Dr. Nathanson lobbied for legal abortion because he had seen many women who had suffered physical damage or death due to illegal abortions. Dr. Nathanson's false statistics helped to convince our citizens that we needed to legalize abortion in our country.

Dr. Nathanson was one of the founders of NARAL (National Abortion and Reproductive Rights Action League. In lobbying for legal abortion Dr. Nathanson admits to using fictional statics to bolster his claims for legal abortion. He highly inflated the statistics on how many illegal abortions were done each year and how many deaths occurred from these illegal abortions.

Once abortion became legal in the State of New York Dr. Nathanson's set up a clinic, and Dr. Nathanson became an abortionist. He and his clinic completed thousands of abortions, and Dr. Nathanson even performed one abortion on a lady that he impregnated.

Since the Row v. Wade Supreme Court decision abortion has become the primary method of birth control in our country.

As technology improved with the invention of ultrasound and the babies could be seen in the womb Dr. Nathanson's acceptance of abortion began to change. He could see the babies in the womb. He realized that this baby is a real human child, and he realized that doctors are suppose to save lives not kill them.

TYPES OF ABORTION

Dilation and Evacuation (D&E): A dilation and evacuation abortion, D&E, is a surgical abortion procedure during which an abortionist first dilates the woman's cervix and then uses instruments to dismember and extract the baby from the uterus. The D&E abortion procedure is usually performed between thirteen and twenty-four weeks.

The abortionist may administer anesthesia. The abortionist then inserts a large suction catheter into the uterus and turns it on, emptying the amniotic fluid.

After the amniotic fluid is removed, the abortionist uses a medical tool—that has rows of sharp "teeth" — to grasp and pull the baby's arms and legs, tearing the limbs from the child's body. The abortionist continues to grasp intestines, spine, heart, lungs, and any other limbs or body parts. The most difficult part of the procedure is usually finding, grasping and crushing the baby's head. After removing pieces of the child's skull, the abortionist uses a curette to scrape the uterus and remove the placenta and any remaining parts of the baby.

The abortionist then collects all of the baby's parts and reassembles them to make sure there are two arms, two legs, and that all of the pieces have been removed. The pieces are assembled on a table and put together like a jigsaw puzzle to insure that the entire baby has been removed. Any parts of the baby left in the womb can be detrimental to the woman's health. One doctor said of D&E that you need a lot of strength to do it – pulling arms and legs off of babies and putting them in a stack on top of a table.

Salt Poisoning: Otherwise known as "saline amniocentesis." This technique is used after 16 weeks of pregnancy, when enough fluid has accumulated in the amniotic fluid sac surrounding the baby.

A needle is inserted through the mother's abdomen and amniotic fluid is withdrawn and replaced with a solution of concentrated salt. The baby breathes in, swallowing the salt, and is poisoned. The chemical solution also causes painful burning and deterioration of the baby's skin. After about an hour, the child dies. The mother goes into labor about 33 to 35 hours after instillation and delivers a dead, burned, and shriveled baby. About 97% of mothers deliver their dead babies within 72 hours.

This procedure can be dangerous to the mother and result in uncontrolled blood clotting throughout the body with severe hemmorhage as well as other serious side effects on the central nervous system. Seizures, coma, or death may also result from saline inadvertently injected into the woman's vascular system.

Partial-Birth Abortion: This procedure is used to abort babies when women who are 20 to 32 weeks pregnant -- or even later into pregnancy. Guided by ultrasound, the abortionist reaches into the uterus, grabs the unborn baby's leg with forceps, and pulls the baby into the birth canal, **except for the head**, which is deliberately kept just inside the womb. At this point in a partial-birth abortion, the baby is alive. Then the abortionist jams scissors into the back of the baby's skull and spreads the tips of the scissors apart to enlarge the wound. After removing the scissors, a suction catheter is inserted into the skull and the baby's brains are sucked out. The collapsed head is then removed from the uterus. Babies born at 23 weeks or more often survive. This procedure eliminates that possibility.

Compare these forms of death with the care given to convicted criminals who receive the death penalty and the care given to them to complete their sentence without being cruel and unusual punishment.

After Dr. Nathanson's conversion to Pro Life instead of Pro Choice he made two graphic videos to show the horrors of the abortion procedure. These can be seen on YouTube. One is called "The Silent Scream" and the other is called "Eclipse of Reason".

WHY

And why do people work in the abortion business - **MONEY!** Much money is to be made killing babies…and much of it is under the table, in cash never reported. Some of the employees at abortion clinics are trained by marketing professionals to actively sell the abortion. Nothing is said at an abortion clinic about adoption, or homes for girls to live in to provide care for them and financial support, or nothing of changing of the mind. Nothing to talk the lady out of getting the abortion—just selling them on getting it. The women were never given any type of alternatives to abortions!

Prior to the abortion all they were told about the procedure itself was that they would experience slight cramping, similar to menstrual cramps. They were not told about the development of the baby, or about the pain that the baby would be experiencing, or about the physical or emotional effects the abortion would have on them.

WHEN FACED WITH REALITY

Many people, doctors, nurses, and employees turn away from the abortion business each year just as Dr. Nathanson did. One such person was Abby Johnson. Abby was the director of a Planned Parenthood clinic in Bryan, Texas. Her clinic was regularly picketed by Pro-Life supporters. Abby herself had two abortions. After seeing an abortion on ultrasound Abby turned to her protesters for help. She left Planned Parenthood and has become an active Pro Life supporter.

A movie about her life is coming out in 2019 titled "Unplanned". This movie will take a little different viewpoint because Abby has been on both sides of the issue — she has had abortions, and she has worked for Planned Parenthood, and now she is Pro Life. The reviews of this movie say it is not an attack movie — its about what is right and wrong. **Isn't that the whole story of abortion!**

There are many others who have worked in the abortion business. They have seen the horror stories that go on inside these clinics. Many have realized how barbaric the abortion is, and they have left their employment because of what they have seen and done. Go to the website "Pro-Life Action League" to the "Meet the Abortion Providers", (*https://prolifeaction.org/former-providers/*), to hear the former employees talk about the abortions and deception that goes on in these clinics.

THE IRONY

What led Dr. Nathanson and Abby Johnson to turn away from abortion is now routinely used in to aid in abortions — the ultrasound. The nurses have to look at the ultrasound picture to gauge how far along the baby is for an abortion, because the larger the pregnancy, the more you get paid. But the women having the abortions are not allowed to see the ultrasound for fear that if they even heard the heartbeat they would not have the abortion.

LIES AND DECEPTION

America's legal and cultural embrace of abortion has been based on lies, deception, greed, and monumental selfishness. From the very beginning of Dr. Nathanson and NARAL used false and misleading statics in trying to get abortion legalized. Before she died Norma McCorvey admitted Roe v. Wade was a fraud, and that she was used by abortion rights attorneys in their quest to legalize the procedure. Planned Parenthood continues to mislead the public in what services it offers, but none of their services are to direct pregnant mothers to help facilities in lieu of abortion.

Abortion is brutal and barbaric. It is murdering the most innocent victim there can be. When faced with the facts and the Word of God how can anyone support this cruel and unusual death to our babies. Some people believe that because it is legal it is OK. How wrong they can be.

Please do not be this person:

"Here I was with no real convictions, caught in the middle. And so I did what a lot of us do throughout our life. We don't do anything. I didn't talk with anybody about it, I didn't talk with my folks about it, I didn't think about it. **I did nothing!**

ABORTION IS MURDER

Here is what God says:

Psalm 139:13-16 (ESV)
13
For you formed my inward parts;
you knitted me together in my mother's womb.
14
I praise you, for I am fearfully and wonderfully made.
Wonderful are your works;
my soul knows it very well.
15
My frame was not hidden from you,
when I was being made in secret,
intricately woven in the depths of the earth.

16
Your eyes saw my unformed substance;
in your book were written, every one of them,
the days that were formed for me,
when as yet there was none of them.

God knit you together in your mothers womb. He formed you from the very beginning of inception! And He knew you!

Folks, abortion is murder, and nothing but murder!

Exodus 20:13 (ESV)
13 *"You shall not murder.*

God is the only one who can give life and the only one who can take life!

Deuteronomy 32:39 (ESV)
39
"'See now that I, even I, am he,
and there is no god beside me;
I kill and I make alive;
I wound and I heal;
and there is none that can deliver out of my hand.

Only God can kill!

And for the ones who perform abortions and who make their living providing abortions:

Genesis 9:5-6 (ESV)
5 *And for your lifeblood <u>I will require a reckoning</u>: from every beast <u>I will require it and from man</u>. From his fellow man I will require a reckoning for the life of man.*

6 *"Whoever sheds the blood of man, by man shall his blood be shed, for God made man in his own image.*

THE HOMOSEXUAL AGENDA

Today, thanks to America's politically correct "gay-friendly" culture, millions of human beings in the grip of this same unnatural sexual compulsion find it much easier to accept. **But they still don't understand it, and they have little desire to understand it.**

Political forces made considerable strides during the '70s in persuading, or intimidating, the American Psychiatric Association into removing homosexuality from its official list of mental disorders.

In 1988 some activists representing homosexual groups from across the nation held a war conference in Virginia to map out their movement's future. The next year a comprehensive public relations plan was put forth by two highly intelligent and educated researchers. They published a book thats theme was to conquer the fear and hatred of homosexuals in America. The goal was to force the acceptance of the homosexual culture into the mainstream, to silence opposition, and ultimately convert American society.

One of their strategies was to replace the word "homosexual" (removing all sexual connotations) and replacing the word with "gay" meaning "happy. Another strategy was to imply that they were being denied the basic freedoms (rights) that of citizenship that others enjoy.

Now all of this was designed to misdirect the public from the realities that homosexuals routinely have hundreds of sexual partners and weird sexual practices. They were told not to talk about these issues. Instead they were told to look and act normal. They wanted to first you get their foot in the door, by being as similar as possible and then when your sexual difference is finally accepted – can you start dragging in your other peculiarities, one by one.

After they began to be accepted the door could be open to sado-masochists, leather fetishists, crossdressers, transgenders, and other "peculiar" members of the homosexual which is exactly what is going on today.

This desensitizing by the homosexual activist is described as inundating the public in a "continuous flood of homosexual-related advertising, presented in the least offensive fashion possible.

In their cultural and political campaigns they have successfully tied all who oppose their agenda to negatives, such as Nazis or bigots. And understand this because you can certainly see this happening in our society today the "homosexual rights" agenda, includes indoctrinating kindergartners with pro-homosexual propaganda. This is extraordinarily subversive to America's foundational values and institutions.

Whereas fifty years ago the portrayal of homosexuality as normal and respectable was unheard of, now we're facing exactly the opposite spectacle. This stunning turnaround is reflected in virtually every area of society. Whether in culture, politics, law, business, the news media, entertainment, education, or **even the church**, homosexual strides have been nothing short of astonishing. Once condemned as "immoral deviants," homosexuals and lesbians today are honored, idealized, defended as victims, and celebrated as role models.

This is particularly disturbing how these influences are effecting the Christian churches today. Too many churches are succumbing to the culture instead of the non-changing Word of God. It is so sad to see this happening in our society and around the world today.

HOMOSEXUALITY THE BIGGER AGENDA

There is one goal of homosexual marriage that I doubt many of the homosexuals even realize. The goal is to eliminate heterosexual marriage. In the countries where homosexual marriage has been legal for a number of years the heterosexual marriage rates are down. They are going down in this country also.

LGBT activist Masha Gessen is a Russian-American journalist, author, translator and activist. In 2012 she gave a speech where she said the push for homosexual marriage has less to do with the right to marry — it is about diminishing and eventually destroying the institution of marriage and redefining the "traditional family". She went on to say homosexual marriage generally involves lying about what we are going to do with marriage when we get there. You can find her making these statements on "YouTube under the headline "Lesbian Speaks Openly About Eradicating Marriage".

What some Americans and some Christians could not foresee was what would happen after the Supreme Court made homosexual marriage legal. Many thought that would make them happy. But that was not all they wanted. The homosexuals want to be loved and accepted by everybody, and don't want to be viewed as sinners. And who thinks they are sinners? Christians! So, now that the Supreme Court said the homosexual marriages are allowed the homosexual activists are constantly attacking Christianity and filing lawsuits.

THE TRUTH ABOUT HOMOSEXUALITY

But what about the truth regarding homosexuality? What about the reality of what causes it, and of what it means physically and spiritually for those so oriented?

Does homosexuality result from childhood sexual molestations? Do these attacks result in internal struggles against homosexual compulsions? There was a time when psychiatry, psychology, religion, and common sense all said "yes." Sexual abuse studies say that young males are "up to 7 times more likely to self-identify as gay or bisexual than peers who had not been abused."

There was a time when most Americans knew that homosexuals were not "born that way" but rather had their normal gender-identity development disturbed and redirected through early childhood experiences. There was a time when we recognized on some level that **unhealthy relationships with mothers and fathers** could cause girls and boys to grow up with gender confusion – just like emotionally devastating traumatic experiences of molestation.

Unfortunately, with all the misleading marketing behind the campaign to mainstream homosexuality, what's been swept under the rug is the recognition – once commonplace in America – that flawed early relationships or sexual victimization can put a child on the road to homosexuality.

Homosexual activist know this. Yet they advise homosexuals to claim they were born homosexual even though they know they were not. They state that for all practical purposes, homosexuals should be considered to have been born gay even though sexual orientation, for most humans, seems to be the product of a complex interaction between innate predispositions and environmental factors during childhood and early adolescence. In reality environmental factors are involved in their decisions to accept homosexuality, but they refuse to admit it publicly. And they refuse to admit this because if they acknowledge the truth it would be understood that homosexuality was a moral choice and would confirm Bible teaching that homosexuality is a sin. Otherwise their actions could rightly be identified as wicked and seductive.

The endgame for the homosexual is not only to bring about the complete acceptance and approval of homosexuality, but also to prohibit and even criminalize public criticism of homosexuality, including the quotation of biblical passages disapproving of homosexuality. In other words, to eliminate the criticism with the force of law. This is already essentially the case in Canada and parts of Scandinavia.

The homosexual activist will not end their campaign until Christians and other traditionalists opposing homosexuality are shut up, discredited, and utterly silenced – and all because of a little factor we've forgotten about: In truth, there is something wrong with homosexuality. It is unnatural and self-destructive, just as we have long understood it.

To the homosexual living in denial even a loving offer of help from a Christian ex-gay ministry or "reparative therapy" counselor to help overcome the homosexual addiction feels like the most vile, abusive hatred. In fact, it's real love – which they misinterpret as hatred and "bigotry" simply because it causes them to confront a truth that is not welcome in them.

HOMOSEXUAL ATTACKS ON CHRISTIANITY

Not only are Christians different from those living in this world those who live in it and follow Satan want to neutralize all Christians. Christians face opposition from the Freedom From Religion Foundation, the Southern Poverty Law Center, Right Wing Watch, American Atheists Organization, and Gay & Lesbian Alliance Against Defamation. These organizations attack our culture and Christianity.

Thank God for the First Liberty Institute that defends Christian rights for free. They defend religious liberty for churches and religious organizations, the military, in schools, and throughout the public arena.

Let's take a look at a few of the attacks on Christianity that have occurred or are occurring in our country at the present time.

- In Bremerton, Washington School District football coach Kennedy was fired for kneeling on the field for a 15 second silent prayer after the players left the field. He was by himself, no one could hear him, and all he did was kneel in prayer.
- Federal Court of Appeals Orders Removal of 90-Year Old Veterans Memorial. In 1925, The American Legion, the largest veterans service organization in the nation, erected the Bladensburg World War I Veterans Memorial in honor of 49 men of Prince George's County, Md., who gave their lives in the First World War while serving in the U.S. armed forces. This complaint was filed by the American Humanist Association, an atheist organization that claims the memorial violates the Establishment Clause of the First Amendment and has gotten a ruling in its favor from the Fourth Circuit Court of Appeals.

- Oscar Rodriguez, Jr., a decorated Air Force veteran was assaulted and forcibly removed from a retirement ceremony over the word "God". In March 2016, Chuck Roberson, a retiring service member, asked Rodriguez to deliver the flag-folding speech at his retirement ceremony, to be held at Travis Air Force Base near Sacramento. Rodriguez agreed, but when he began the speech, uniformed Airmen assaulted and forcibly removed him from Roberson's retirement ceremony because the speech included the word "God."
- Churches Impacted by hurricanes Harvey and Irma Receive FEMA Aid Case. Trump administration ends policy prohibiting houses of worship from receiving FEMA aid after receiving letter from First Liberty. Late in the summer of 2017, Hurricane Harvey pummeled parts of Texas and Louisiana for days with record-breaking flooding. On its heels came Hurricane Irma, devastating areas of Florida with severe winds and more flooding. Among the tens of thousands affected were hundreds, possibly thousands of churches, temples, synagogues, and other religious organizations. This is because FEMA's Public Assistance Program and Policy Guide misinterprets the Stafford Act. The Stafford Act contains a nondiscrimination clause that mandates the President must protect religious entities from discrimination when it comes to relief assistance. On September 20, 2017, First Liberty Institute sent a letter to FEMA, pointing out that President Trump could easily correct this discriminatory policy. Doing so would help secure much-needed federal assistance for houses of worship and religious nonprofits, many of which are already sacrificing what little they have left to help their own communities. By January 2, 2018, FEMA announced that it would expand its guidelines to include houses of worship among those eligible to receive disaster relief.

- Sterling V. United States - U.S. Marine convicted at a court martial for refusing to remove Bible verse in her workspace. United States Marine Corps Lance Corporal (LCpl) Monifa Sterling was convicted at a court-martial after she refused to take down Bible verses she had posted in her workspace and for reposting the verses after her supervisor threw them in the trash. A trial court ruled against Sterling, giving her a bad conduct discharge and reducing her rank. Sterling appealed to the Navy-Marine Corps Court of Criminal Appeals, but the appeals court also ruled against her. First Liberty Institute stepped in and appealed Sterling's case to the Court of Appeals for the Armed Forces (CAAF)— the highest military court. On August 10, 2016, the CAAF ruled against Sterling, denying her constitutional right to religious freedom. First Liberty appealed the decision to the U.S. Supreme Court on December 23, 2016, and it was announced on June 5, 2017, that the Court declined to review the case.
- Alexia Palma Case. A Houston health care company fires young Catholic immigrant for being unwilling to promote contraception. Alexia Palma is a young Catholic immigrant from Guatemala who worked at a Houston inner-city health clinic. There, she taught several classes, including a short course on "Becoming a Mom." One of the classes in the course was about birth control. Because the Catholic Church opposes birth control, Alexia asked for a simple religious accommodation to show a video instead of teaching the class. This worked well for approximately 18 months. But when new management came in, they gave her an ultimatum – "put aside" her "personal beliefs" and teach the class, or else be terminated. Even though teaching the class constituted less than 2% of her job, and even though other employees volunteered to teach the class for her, the new management refused to consider a religious accommodation and fired her. On December 21, 2016,

First Liberty Institute filed a complaint with the U.S. Equal Employment Opportunity Commission charging Alexia's employer, Legacy Community Health (LCH), with religious discrimination. On May 9, 2017, First Liberty announced an amicable settlement with Legacy.

- Dr. Eric Walsh Case, State of Georgia fires public health official over sermons. Dr. Eric Walsh is an expert in public health with multiple advanced degrees. He has served as the director of the City of Pasadena's Public Health Department, was appointed to President Obama's Presidential Advisory Council on HIV/AIDs and also served as an associate pastor for his church. In May 2014, the State of Georgia's Department of Public Health hired Dr. Walsh as a District Health Director. But soon after Dr. Walsh accepted the offer, state officials asked him to submit recordings of his sermons for their review. After inspecting his sermons, they fired him. First Liberty Institute filed a lawsuit against the State of Georgia on behalf of Dr. Walsh, contending that no one should be fired from his job for something he said in a sermon. In February 2017, the State of Georgia paid $225,000 to settle Dr. Walsh's religious discrimination lawsuit.

- Kelvin J. Cochran is an author, public speaker, former Administrator of the United States Fire Administration appointed by President Obama, and former Fire Chief of Atlanta Fire Department. He was fired from the Atlanta fire department after he wrote a book for members of his church expressing biblical views on sexuality, adultery, and homosexuality. Cochran was suspended for 30 days without pay starting November 24, 2014 for distributing to employees a book he had written, Who Told You That You Were Naked?, which expressed Cochran's religious views which included calling homosexuality and lesbianism a perversion and which mayor Kasim Reed considered to be discriminatory against LGBT people. On January 6, 2015, after returning from the suspension, he was informed that he would have to resign or be terminated. On December 20th, 2017, United States District Court Judge Leigh Martin May upheld his firing and also ruled that as an "at-will" employee, his firing was legal. The City's pre-clearance rules on employee outside activities were, however, ruled unconstitutional. On October 15th, 2018, the City Council agreed to pay Cochran $1.2 million dollars as compensation for damages and attorney's fees.

Folks, these are just a few of the examples of the way Christians and Christianity are being attacked by our culture every day. Florists, bakers, photographers are being attacked for their Christian faith and their opposition to same sex marriage. Barronelle Stutzman, a florist in Washington state, was taken to court by a homosexual man whom she called a friend and had been a customer of hers for nine years.

Jack Phillips, a baker in Denver, was taken to the Supreme Court for refusing to bake a cake for a homosexual wedding. This case was won by Phillips attorneys. After this ruling the Colorado government filed on him again for refusing to make a cake for transgenders. These attacks will not stop. **We as Christians must defend our faith!**

Go to Christian web news sites and you can keep up with these types of attacks. Look at the Christian Post, the Gospel Herald, WND, Faithwire, Charisma News, and One News Now. Go to the web site American Family Radio, a Christian based radio and internet news and programs. Listen to your local Christian radio stations for Christian music and programs from well know established ministers across the country.

Homosexuality Is A Sin

Leviticus 18:22 (ESV)
22 *You shall not lie with a male as with a woman; it is an abomination.*

Romans 1:26-28 (ESV)
26 *For this reason God gave them up to dishonorable passions. For their women exchanged natural relations for those that are contrary to nature;* **27** *and the men likewise gave up natural relations with women and were consumed with passion for one another, men committing shameless acts with men and receiving in themselves the due penalty for their error.*
28 *And since they did not see fit to acknowledge God, God gave them up to a debased mind to do what ought not to be done.*

1 Timothy 1:8-11 (ESV)
8 *Now we know that the law is good, if one uses it lawfully,* **9** *understanding this, that the law is not laid down for the just but for the lawless and disobedient, for the ungodly and sinners, for the unholy and profane, for those who strike their fathers and mothers, for murderers,* **10** *the sexually immoral, men who practice homosexuality, enslavers, liars, perjurers, and whatever else is contrary to sound doctrine,* **11** *in accordance with the gospel of the glory of the blessed God with which I have been entrusted.*

Because Jesus was hated we will be hated:

Matthew 10:22 (ESV)
22 *and you will be hated by all for my name's sake. But the one who endures to the end will be saved.*

John 15:18-25 (ESV) The Hatred of the World
18 *"If the world hates you, know that it has hated me before it hated you.* **19** *If you were of the world, the world would love you as its own; but because you are not of the world, but I chose you out of the world, therefore the world hates you.* **20** *Remember the word that I said to you: 'A servant is not greater than his master.' If they persecuted me, they will also persecute you. If they kept my word, they will also keep yours.* **21** *But all these things they will do to you on account of*

my name, because they do not know him who sent me. **22** *If I had not come and spoken to them, they would not have been guilty of sin, but now they have no excuse for their sin.* **23** *Whoever hates me hates my Father also.* **24** *If I had not done among them the works that no one else did, they would not be guilty of sin, but now they have seen and hated both me and my Father.* **25** *But the word that is written in their Law must be fulfilled: 'They hated me without a cause.'*

In hating what God hates I used the scripture in Proverbs 8:13:

Proverbs 8:13 ESV
"The fear of the Lord is hatred of evil. Pride and arrogance and the way of evil and perverted speech I hate".

God uses the word "pride" in this verse. Pride is one major cause of many different types of sin, but note how the homosexuals have adopted that word — "Gay Pride"!

CHAPTER 6

POLITICS, COURTS, AND ELECTIONS

Proverbs 14:34 (ESV)
34 *Righteousness exalts a nation, but sin is a reproach to any people.*

I believe this is one of the most important chapters in my book. The courts, politics, and elections are where Christians can, and should be, extremely involved in to protect our religious liberties that we have had since the founders of our country gave us these rights.

Proverbs and Politics

In America government is "of the people, by the people, and for the people." In Proverbs (and the New Testament as well, Rom. 13:1-7) the king was responsible before God to punish evildoers and to reward the righteous. **It is every American who bears this responsibility in our nation**. Our government is representative and so we elect officials who act in our behalf. **While some Christians may be called of God to run for political office, we all have the right, <u>and the responsibility</u>, to help elect those who will govern <u>righteously</u>**. When our officials fail to keep this trust we have an obligation to seek to change their minds or to work to replace them. Since it is we, then, who are responsible to rule, let us look carefully at the teaching of Proverbs on the relationship between righteousness and ruling.

Good government is a godly government according to Proverbs. Righteous is defined as acting in an upright, moral way; virtuous. Government should be righteous according to Proverbs:

Proverbs 14:34 (ESV)
34 *Righteousness exalts a nation, but sin is a reproach to any people.*

Proverbs 29:2 (ESV)
2 *When the righteous increase, the people rejoice, but when the wicked rule, the people groan.*

Proverbs 11:10-11 (ESV)
10 *When it goes well with the righteous, the city rejoices, and when the wicked perish there are shouts of gladness.* **11** *By the blessing of the upright a city is exalted, but by the mouth of the wicked it is overthrown.*

The point of these Proverbs is that righteousness is not only right, it is best. When righteousness is promoted and preserved by government, the people are blessed.

When government fails to achieve its intended purpose, the people suffer.

A righteous leader will seek the truth:

Proverbs 28:5 (ESV)
5 *Evil men do not understand justice, but those who seek the Lord understand it completely.*

While there may be wisdom in separating certain religious functions from political office, there is no way that we can separate righteousness from political office. If the purpose of government is to promote righteousness and to punish evil, how can we avoid defining righteousness and defending it as a part of our political obligation before God?

Those in positions of power sometimes thwart justice by showing deference to certain individuals in the community. Proverbs condemns such partiality and insists upon justice and equity.

Proverbs 17:23 (ESV)
23 *The wicked accepts a bribe in secret to pervert the ways of justice.*

Proverbs 18:5 (ESV)
5 *It is not good to be partial to the wicked or to deprive the righteous of justice.*

Righteousness is often evidenced by one's response to wickedness. The righteous ruler will not tolerate sin. He will not practice wickedness, nor will he tolerate its practice or presence. He seeks it out and deals justly with it.

A big problem in our culture, and it is increasing, is the lack of society to punish criminals. Proverbs warns us that if we take a soft position on sin we do a disservice to the criminal by encouraging him to repeat his crime. This is one reason our recidivist rate is so high.

Proverbs 19:19 (ESV)
19 *A man of great wrath will pay the penalty, for if you "deliver" him, you will only have to do it again.*

In the NASB AND NLT Bible versions "rescue" is used in place of "deliver". In other words if a punishment is not given to the offender he will repeat his criminal ways.

Power, political or otherwise, is given by God so that we may serve others. When we forget this we are in danger of being set aside.

Government is to function so that the righteous are rewarded, the evil are punished, and the rights of the helpless are protected.

Hate what God hates!

Romans 12:9 (ESV)
9 Let love be genuine. Abhor what is evil; hold fast to what is good.

Psalm 97:10 (ESV)
"O you who love the Lord, hate evil!"

The only things we should hate are the very things God hates. The Bible tells us there is a time to hate:

Ecclesiastes 3:8 (ESV)
a time to love, and a time to hate;
a time for war, and a time for peace

Proverbs 6:16-19 (ESV)
"There are <u>six things that the Lord hates</u>, seven that are an abomination to him: haughty eyes, a lying tongue, and <u>hands that shed innocent blood</u>, a heart that devises wicked plans, feet that make haste to run to evil, a false witness who breathes out lies, and one who sows discord among brothers".

Psalm 97:10 (ESV)
O you who love the Lord, <u>hate evil</u>!
He preserves the lives of his saints;
he delivers them from the hand of the wicked.

Proverbs 8:13 ESV
"The fear of the Lord is hatred of evil. Pride and arrogance and the way of evil and perverted speech I hate".

The Bible is full of messages on love. Love the Lord, love your neighbor, etc. In this book I have stressed and will continue to express the reason we are on this earth. To give glory and honor to God. To prepare our lives to live in Heaven with God eternally. In doing this we will be obedient to God and living as an example in Him. In living for God we will love what the Lord loves, and we will hate what God hates. In living our lives for God the choices we make in politics and elections we should love what God loves and hate what God hates. **Our votes should be based on God's words.**

This brings me to the state of our culture today. In the last 60 years our country has been on a steady road of decline, or even a roller coaster of decline. As I stated in the first paragraph of this book this information is extremely important to the Millennial generation and those younger. I was born in the Baby Boomer generation. My generation has the clearest vision to see how our nation has slithered into decline. My generation is old enough to have witnessed the most dramatic, climactic points in our country's direction. We can look back and see their impact upon our culture. We can see how so many court decisions have hurt our country and contributed to its decline.

Ecclesiastes 3:16 (ESV)
16 *Moreover, I saw under the sun that in the place of justice, even there was wickedness, and in the place of righteousness, even there was wickedness.*

Proverbs 17:15 Version (ESV)
He who justifies the wicked and he who condemns the righteous are both alike an abomination to the Lord.

Reference the verse from Ecclesiastes the (NLT) New Living Translation of the Bible refers to the place of justice and righteousness as the courts. Wickedness and corruption sit in the place where justice and righteousness should be, thus tainting the legal system. Is there anything more outrageous than the miscarriage of justice in the court of law? God certainly is outraged at the decisions that are coming from the courts. God does not ignore injustice. He will bring it to an end at His appointed time.

Now, let's take a look at what has happened in the last sixty years. First let's look at one court opinion that has been a big factor in leading to our nation's decline.

Separation of Church and State

The attack on separation of church and state involves twisting words and reading history backwards, and it involves making an inconvenient part of the Constitution disappear. Most ardently espoused by loud foes of "big government," the attack aims to place government in charge of Americans' spiritual lives.

"Separation of church and state" is a common statement that you frequently hear. This is incorrectly used today meaning the church should stay out of the state's business and the state staying out of the church's business. Most people incorrectly think the phrase is in the constitution.

The phrase "wall of separation between the church and the state" was originally coined by Thomas Jefferson in a letter to the Danbury Baptists on January 1, 1802. His purpose in this letter was to appease the fears of the Danbury, Connecticut Baptists, and so he told them that this wall had been erected to protect them. **The metaphor was used exclusively to keep the state out of the church's business, not to keep the church out of the state's business.**

The constitution states, "Congress shall make no law respecting an establishment of religion, or prohibiting the free exercise thereof." Both the free exercise clause and the establishment clause place restrictions on the government concerning laws they pass or interfering with religion. **No restrictions are placed on religions except that a religious denomination cannot become the state religion.**

Jefferson's words have been twisted to keep for the church out of the state's business. This makes the "separation of church and state" metaphor an icon for eliminating anything having to do with Christian theism, the religion of our heritage, in the public arena.

This misinterpretation has led to many lawsuits to eliminate any type of Christian identification, and many judicial decisions to be improperly imposed.

The Supreme Court thoroughly studied this issue, and in 1892 gave what is known as the Trinity Decision. In that decision the Supreme Court declared, "this is a Christian nation." Our nation reflects these values in numerous ways in our capitol and country:

- Emblazoned over the Speaker of the House in the US Capitol are the words "In God We Trust."
- The Supreme Court building built in the 1930's has carvings of Moses and the Ten Commandments.
- God is mentioned in stone all over Washington D.C., on its monuments and buildings.
- As a nation, we have celebrated Christmas to commemorate the Savior's birth for centuries.
- Oaths in courtrooms have invoked God from the beginning.
- The founding fathers often quoted the Bible in their writings.
- Every president that has given an inaugural address has mentioned God in that speech.
- Prayers have been said at the swearing in of each president.
- Each president was sworn in on the Bible, saying the words, "So help me God."
- Our national anthem mentions God.
- The liberty bell has a Bible verse engraved on it. (Leviticus 25:10)
- The original constitution of all 50 states mentions God.

- Chaplains have been in the public payroll from the very beginning.
- Our nations birth certificate, the Declaration of Independence, mentions God four times.
- The Bible was used as a textbook in the schools.

Our nation is deeply rooted in Christianity. So let's look at some of the court rulings that have attacked Christianity in my baby boomer generation.

Court Cases That Have Helped Destroy Religious Liberty in America

1962 — Prayer is removed from the schools (Engel v. Vitale)

1963 — Bible reading is removed from the schools (Abington School District v. Schempp)

1973 — The murder of unborn babies is legalized (Roe v. Wade)

1980 — The Ten Commandments are removed from classrooms (Stone v. Graham)

1992 — Invocations/benedictions are banned from school activities (Lee v. Weisman)

2003 — Sodomy laws declared illegal by the Supreme Court (Lawrence v. Texas)

2005 — Display of the Ten Commandments is ruled unconstitutional (McCreary County v. ACLU of Kentucky)

2013 — Defense of Marriage Act (DOMA) is declared unconstitutional (United States v. Windsor)

2015 — Same-sex marriage is approved by the Supreme Court (Obergefell v. Hodges)

In 1962 prayer was removed from public schools. In 1963 Bible reading was banned in public schools. In 1973 abortion is legalized. Two thousand and three brought the end to the laws against sodomy, and in 2015 the legalization of homosexual marriage.

ABORTION & HOMOSEXUALITY

I covered these subjects of abortion and homosexuality in the chapter titled Our Culture.

In this chapter I want you to see how important these issues are when it comes to electing the leaders of our country.

First let's look at the 2003 Supreme Court decision striking down sodomy laws in Texas and 13 other states. These laws were obviously written to deter homosexuality. These laws were called "sodomy" based on the bible record of the cities Sodom and Gomorrah. God destroyed these cities for their evil and immoral and perverted sexual activities. These cities were so evil and immoral that no righteous person could be found. Not even ten in the city! God rescued only Lot and his family, Abraham's nephew. Sexual immorality had taken over the whole city. This is happening in our country today!

So how does abortion and homosexuality fit in to our election process in America today?

ELECTIONS

Now let's look at the 2016 Presidential election and future elections to come.

Romans 13:1 (ESV)
13 *Let every person be subject to the governing authorities. For there is no authority except from God, and those that exist have been instituted by God.*

There is no authority except from God, and those that exist have been instituted by God. This means that no one has ever been President of the United States, or leader of any country, without God wanting him there. This certainly includes Barack Obama, Bill Clinton, George W. Bush, Richard Nixon, and of course Donald Trump. President Trump received 83% of the Christian vote, but why. That is my main point in this chapter. Why was Donald Trump elected President of the United States?

Much of the time the voters don't know anything about the person they vote for. I believe wholeheartedly that the main reason Barack Obama was elected was because of his race. I heard many young Americans simply say they were voting for him because it was time to have an African American president. So what was the deciding factor for the victory of Mr. Trump.

The democratic party began to shape into the party they are in the 2012 presidential campaign. During the 2012 Democratic Convention the party platform that was drawn up failed to mention any reference to God. Methodist Minister and Governor of Ohio Ted Strickland introduced an amendment on the floor to reinsert the language invoking God and recognizing Jerusalem as Israel's capital. The Convention Chairman Antonio Villaraigosa put the amendment to a voice vote requiring a two-thirds majority for passage. The vocal vote was too difficult to determine "ayes" or "nays" because it was so close, and in no way was a two-thirds majority obtained. The Chairman held this vocal vote three times. After the third time a lady standing next to the chairman said he had to rule. The chairman then declared the amendment had passed meaning God would be added to their platform. This inclusion of putting God back into the democratic platform resulted in a loud eruption of boos. This vote can also be found and seen on YouTube.

Hillary Clinton made her opinion known on April 23, 2015 in a speech delivered at the Women's World Summit. In this speech she said, "Laws have to be backed up with resources and political will. And deep-seated religious beliefs have to be changed." Folks the Bible, the Word of God was written for all times. Nothing needs to be changed in religious beliefs. You can see and hear Hillary Clinton's comments on YouTube.

There are probably many reasons why Mr. Trump won, but I believe that each and every Christian should vote honoring God. By this I mean "Hate What God Hates".

In 2016 many pastors spoke out on this election. What they said was "look at the party platforms".

THE PLATFORMS

The Presidential Election of 2016 was the most important election of my lifetime. When you look at the platforms of 2016 this is what you will find:

Sanctity of Life

Democrat Platform - Democrats seek to repeal the Hyde Amendment so that federal funds can be used to pay for abortions. The platform says, "We will continue to stand up to Republican efforts to defund Planned Parenthood health centers."

Republican Platform - The GOP asserts the sanctity of human life and affirms, *"The unborn child has a fundamental right to life which cannot be infringed."* The party supports a Human Life Amendment making clear that the 14th Amendment's protections apply to children before birth, and it salutes states that require informed consent, parental consent, waiting periods and clinic regulation.

On Marriage:

Democrat Platform - Democrats applaud the Supreme court ruling on LGBT Marriage

Republican Platform - The GOP condemns the Supreme Court ruling.

Israel & Jerusalem:

Democrat Platform - The platform states: "We will always support Israel's right to defend itself, including by retaining it qualitative military edge, and oppose any effort to delegitimize Israel. .... While

Jerusalem is a matter for final status negotiations, it should remain the capital of Israel, and undivided city accessible to people of all faiths.

Republican Platform - Republicans express *"unequivocal support for Israel,"* pointing out that it is the only Middle Eastern country with freedom of speech and freedom of religion. The GOP recognizes "Jerusalem as the eternal and indivisible capital of the Jewish state." The party opposes the U.N.'s treatment of Israel as a pariah state.

I have listed three issues which concerns Christians. I have previously mentioned Israel so let me touch on that issue. Israel is God's chosen people. Israel is to be supported. In speaking of Israel God said:

Genesis 12:3 (ESV)
3 *I will bless those who bless you, and him who dishonors you I will curse, and in you all the families of the earth shall be blessed."*

Barack Obama treated Israel and Benjamin Netanyahu terribly when he was president. He even had people in Israel trying to get Mr. Netanyahu defeated in his election.

In regards to the election and voting for a candidate or party that supports abortion, protestants and Catholics expressed concern of this election. Below is a quote from a Catholic priest published on CNS News.

Catholic Priest: 'Your Soul Will Be In Grave Danger'

If You Vote For Pro-Abortion Politicians

By Michael W. Chapman | October 11, 2016 | 12:29 PM EDT

"Make no mistake!" said Fr. Lankeit, the pastor of the Saints Simon & Jude Cathedral in Phoenix, Ariz. "There is no single issue that threatens innocent human life more directly, consistently, imminently and urgently than the deliberate killing of baby boys and baby girls in their mother's womb. **No issue!**"

HATE WHAT GOD HATES

Do you think God hates abortion? The direct and intentional murder of a child for convenience of the others.

Do you think God hates homosexuality? The word He uses in an abomination. The sexual perversion of the human bodies.

Romans 1:21-27 (ESV)
21 For although they knew God, they did not honor him as God or give thanks to him, but they became futile in their thinking, and their foolish hearts were darkened.
22 Claiming to be wise, they became fools, 23 and exchanged the glory of the immortal God for images resembling mortal man and birds and animals and creeping things.
24 Therefore God gave them up in the lusts of their hearts to impurity, to the dishonoring of their bodies among themselves, 25 because they exchanged the truth about God for a lie and worshiped and served the creature rather than the Creator,
who is blessed forever! Amen.
26 For this reason God gave them up to dishonorable passions. For their women exchanged natural relations for those that are contrary to nature; 27 and the men likewise gave up natural relations with women and were consumed with passion for one another, men committing shameless acts with men and receiving in themselves the due penalty for their error.

How can a Christian vote for any person or party that endorses and encourages these kind of actions?

Can you see Jesus today walking into a voting booth and pulling the lever for a person or party that endorses abortion?

Can you see Jesus today walking into a voting booth and pulling the lever for a person or party that endorses homosexual weddings?

If we truly call ourselves Christians, we must not only love what God loves, but we must hate what God hates. This does not give us license to ever act hateful towards any individual; in fact we must love them deeper. It is the kindness of God that draws people into repentance.

But we also cannot turn a blind eye towards the truths explicitly laid out for us in scripture. We can no longer sit on our hands on these issues. It is time to wake up and speak up! Let us love more fiercely than we have ever before and let us pray for our nation as if our lives depended on it. Because they do. They really do.

Please don't take the opinion that there are issues on the ballot other than abortion or homosexual rights. No issue should give precedence as to what is opposed to God!

HATE WHAT GOD HATES

I pray that you can see the downturn that has affected this country since the baby boomer years. The USA and the world is spiraling deeper and deeper into immorality and sin, deeper in disrespect for God.

The changes in our world:

What was once condemned is now CELEBRATED - HOMOSEXUALITY

What was celebrated is now CONDEMNED - TRADITIONAL MARRIAGE

Those refusing to celebrate are CONDEMNED - THOSE NOT CELEBRATING HOMOSEXUAL MARRIAGE

Can you see Jesus attending or celebrating a homosexual marriage?

Can you see Jesus going to an "R" rated movie?

Can you see see Jesus speaking profanity?

Hate what God hates! Hate everything God hates. A Christian cannot condone sin or make excuses for sin because God hates sin! Jesus is calling you out of a world of delusion and deception in which evil is called good and good is called evil.

Isaiah 5:20 (ESV)

20
Woe to those who call evil good and good evil,
who put darkness for light and light for darkness,
who put bitter for sweet and sweet for bitter!

Ephesians 5:11 (ESV)

11 *Take no part in the unfruitful works of darkness, but instead expose them.*

This verse in Ephesians tells us to take no part of the darkness - the evil. Instead expose them. We are to expose evil folks. This has been a major fault over these last 60 years when the Christians looked the other way when this evil was being spread.

James 4:4 (ESV)

4 *You adulterous people! Do you not know that friendship with the world is enmity with God? Therefore whoever wishes to be a friend of the world makes himself an enemy of God.*

A true believer submits to the righteousness of God. He abandons all hope in himself and his own righteousness, and rests wholly in the righteousness of Christ for his acceptance before God. A true believer rests in Christ and Him only as his Savior. A true believer can't be neutral on these matters. **A true believer votes for righteousness!**

CHAPTER 7

PROPHECY

1 Thessalonians 4:16-18 (ESV)
16 For the Lord himself will descend from heaven with a cry of command, with the voice of an archangel, and with the sound of the trumpet of God. And the dead in Christ will rise first. 17 Then we who are alive, who are left, will be caught up together with them in the clouds to meet the Lord in the air, and so we will always be with the Lord. 18 Therefore encourage one another with these words.

The Bible is 27% prophecy. Prophecy fulfilled to this point include:

Messiah was to be born in Bethlehem.
The Messiah's birth was written in Micah 5:2 seven hundreds years before Christ was born. This is especially prophetic to me because Mary and Joseph did not live in Bethlehem.

Micah 5:2 (ESV)
2
But you, O Bethlehem Ephrathah,
who are too little to be among the clans of Judah,
from you shall come forth for me
one who is to be ruler in Israel,

whose coming forth is from of old,
from ancient days.

Messiah was to die by crucifixion.

Written 1400 years before Christ was born is the prophecy that Christ would die on the cross.

Deuteronomy 21:22-23 (ESV)
22 *"And if a man has committed a crime punishable by death and he is put to death, and you hang him on a tree,* **23** *his body shall not remain all night on the tree, but you shall bury him the same day, for a hanged man is cursed by God. You shall not defile your land that the Lord your God is giving you for an inheritance.*

This prophecy about the Messiah predicts the way in which the Savior would die and the length of time he would remain on the cross. The penalty of death by crucifixion had not been invented, discovered, or used at the time Moses wrote Deuteronomy.

Psalms 22 written by King David 1000 years before Christ has numerous prophecies about the crucifixion of Jesus. Among them is verse 18 it says:

Psalm 22:18 (ESV)
they divide my garments among them,
and for my clothing they cast lots.

This prophecy is fulfilled in Matthew 27:35.

Matthew 27:35 (ESV)
35 *And when they had crucified him, they divided his garments among them by casting lots.*

Arrival of the Messiah.

To me, one of the most impressive prophecies is from Daniel 9 where it tells of the exact arrival of Christ:

Prophecy of the first arrival of Jesus Christ our Messiah:

As a result of the Babylonian invasion the city of Jerusalem and the Temple were completely destroyed in 586 b.c

In this chapter nine of Daniel, he is aware of the prophecy in Jeremiah that the Jews would be held in captivity in Babylon for 70 years. He knew that the seventy years were complete. In his prayers Daniel was asking God for the restoration of Jerusalem.

As Daniel was praying the angel, Gabriel, came to him. He had come to show Daniel what was necessary to understand the entire matter of Israel's program, and specifically, to consider the vision of the seventy weeks described in the verses which follow. Gabriel bears witness to the special relationship which Daniel had to the Lord in that he was one "greatly beloved."

Beginning in Daniel 9 verse 24 Gabriel tells Daniel the future:

Daniel 9:24-27 ESV
24 "Seventy weeks are decreed about your people and your holy city, to finish the transgression, to put an end to sin, and to atone for iniquity, to bring in everlasting righteousness, to seal both vision and prophet, and to anoint a most holy place. **25** *Know therefore and understand that from the going out of the word to restore and build Jerusalem to the coming of an anointed one, a prince, there shall be seven weeks. Then for sixty-two weeks it shall be built again with squares and moat, but in a troubled time.* **26** *And after the sixty-two weeks, an anointed one shall be cut off and shall have nothing. And the people of the prince who is to come shall destroy the city and the sanctuary. Its end shall come with a flood, and to the end there shall be war. Desolations are decreed.* **27** *And he shall make a strong covenant with many for one week, and for half of the week he shall put an*

end to sacrifice and offering. And on the wing of abominations shall come one who makes desolate, until the decreed end is poured out on the desolator."

[First for clarification "weeks": The word "weeks" in Hebrew refers to a unit of seven, or a heptad (*a group of seven*), with its meaning determined by the context. Sometimes it refers to a period of seven days but here it denotes a period of seven years.]

In these verses Gabriel describes the prophecy of 70 Weeks. These weeks are divided into three sections - one of seven weeks, one of 62 weeks, and one of a single week. Each week being of seven years. So the first seven equals 49 years, the next 434 years, and the last of seven years. These all total to 490 years.

Also in these verses Gabriel mentions in verse 25 the coming of the anointed one (Jesus). The first two sets of weeks, seven and sixty-two, were for the restoration of Jerusalem and the rebuilding of the Temple, and the coming of the anointed one — Jesus in 483 years.

The most likely starting point was Artaxerxes' second decree in 444 BC, authorizing Nehemiah to rebuild the walls of Jerusalem (Neh 2:1-8). This decree fits the requirement of the prediction since it was indeed for the restoration of Jerusalem. Moreover, the restoration was carried out in times of distress just as Daniel predicted (v. 25) and Nehemiah described (Nehemiah 4:1–6:14).

The calculation of the prophecy is as follows: There will be a period of seven weeks of years (49 years) followed by sixty-two weeks of years (434 years), making a total of 69 weeks of years or 483 years from the decree until the coming of the Anointed One, our Messiah. The total of 483 years (69 weeks) should be calculated as specific biblical/prophetic years of 360 days each, according to the Hebrew calendar. The starting point of the prophecy would have begun on Nisan 1 (March 5), 444 BC, followed by 69 weeks of 360 day years or 173,880 days, and culminated on Nisan 10 (March 30), AD 33, the date of Jesus the Messiah's triumphal entry riding on a donkey going into Jerusalem (Lk 19:28-40).

The reason the 69 weeks were divided into two continuous periods was to recognize the purpose of the original decree (**to restore and rebuild Jerusalem**) and identify the completion of the rebuilding of Jerusalem at the end of the seven weeks of years.

The second feature of the prophecy is to predict several events that would follow the seven weeks and the sixty-two weeks (or the total of 69 weeks). First, the Messiah would be cut off, a prediction of the death of the Messiah. Thus, the book of Daniel, written in the sixth century BC, contains predictions not only of the precise date of the Messiah's coming (9:25) but also of the Messiah's death sometime before the destruction of Jerusalem in AD 70. This was fulfilled when Jesus the Messiah was crucified in AD 33.

These verses in Daniel 9:24-27 also describe the people of the prince who is to come. The prince who is to come is distinct from Messiah the Prince but instead is a reference to the future ruler described as the little horn in Daniel 7, also known as the beast or the antichrist.

There is a significant time gap from the end of the 69th week to the beginning of the 70th week, as is common in prophecy. The beginning of the 70th week is yet future, and will be the Tribulation years as describe in Revelation and other scriptures.

Much of the prophecy has come to fruition and much more is to come. The verses quoted at the top the page from 1 Thessalonians refers to what Bible scholars call the Rapture. Among Bible scholars there are differences in belief as to when the rapture may occur, but most scholars believe the rapture is the next prophecy to come true.

The Rapture

1 Corinthians 15:51-52 (ESV)
51 *Behold! I tell you a mystery. We shall not all sleep, but we shall all be changed,* **52** *in a moment, in the twinkling of an eye, at the last trumpet. For the trumpet will sound, and the dead will be raised imperishable, and we shall be changed.*

The word rapture does not appear in the Bible. It come from Paul's First letter to the Thessalonians, where he uses the Greek *harpazo* (ἀρπάζω), meaning to snatch away or seize.

The word rapture is a term frequently used in conjunction with events relating to the Second Coming of Jesus. The meaning or definition of rapture is the idea that the coming of Jesus will take place in two separate stages. The first will be a secret rapture—or carrying away of the saved to heaven—at the beginning of a seven-year period of tribulation, during which the antichrist will appear. The second phase occurs at the close of this time of tribulation when Jesus will return to Earth in triumph and glory.

Many prominent bible scholars and well known pastors believe that the Rapture could come at any time, and that this world as we know it is at the end times.

Let me show you why they have this opinion.
Jesus describes the end times in Matthew 24.

Matthew 24:3 (ESV)
3 *As he sat on the Mount of Olives, the disciples came to him privately, saying, "Tell us, when will these things be, and what will be the sign of your coming and of the end of the age?"*

<u>Continuing in Matthew 24 verses 4 through 31 Jesus goes on to tell the disciples what will come about in the end times, and in verses 32-34 He tells us when the time is near:</u>

Matthew 24:32-33 (ESV)
32 "From the fig tree learn its lesson: as soon as its branch becomes tender and puts out its leaves, you know that summer is near. 33 So also, when you see all these things, you know that he is near, at the very gates. 34 Truly, I say to you, this generation will not pass away until all these things take place.

The fig tree is Israel. In 1948 Israel was not much more than a barren waste land. Today Israel has bloomed. It is the 8th most powerful nation on earth. It has made tremendous strides in many different fields, and it is becoming extremely wealthy.

So the fig tree is blooming and Jesus tells us the time is near. He says no one will know the day or hour, but He wraps it up this way:

Matthew 24:34 (ESV)
34 *Truly, I say to you, this generation will not pass away until all these things take place.*

One of the biggest questions is when does the generation begins that He is talking about, and how long is a generation?

Some believe that the generation would have begun in 1948 when prophecy came true that Israel became a nation again. Others believe the prophecy may have begun in 1967 when Israel regained control of Jerusalem. I believe that both of these incidents could have began the generation that Jesus refers to in His prophecy from Matthew 24:34.

Now, how long is a generation. Of course there are going to be many opinions on this also. The Bible does give life spans that can be used for their opinions. My opinion, and again I am not a Bible scholar, is found in Genesis. If you look at **Genesis 15** you see God talking to Abram. **In verse 13 God tells Abram this**:

13 *Then the Lord said to Abram, "Know for certain that your offspring will be sojourners in a land that is not theirs and will be servants there, and they will be afflicted for four hundred years.*

This verse refers to the Jews being slaves in Egypt for 400 years.

In verse 16 it says:
16 *And they shall come back here in the fourth generation, for the iniquity of the Amorites is not yet complete."*

So God tells Abram that the Jews will be slaves and they would return to the land where God sent Abram (Israel) after 400 years in which He says in verse 16 is the fourth generation. So my guess is that a generation, according to God, is 100 years. If that is a correct assumption on my part that would mean that Jesus would be returning before 2048 or 2067. I'm not setting dates, just time frames. Jesus said we will not know the date or time, but we can know the season of His return.

OK, what was Jesus talking about in Matthew 24:34 when He said "this generation will not pass away until all these things take place"? Look at the prophecies below to see what has to take place before Jesus returns:

<u>**Prophecy of the end times is written in the Old Testament as well as the New Testament**</u>

Let's look at some of these prophecies.
In Isaiah 66:7-8 we read:

Isaiah 66:7-8 New Living Translation (NLT)
7
"Before the birth pains even begin,
Jerusalem gives birth to a son.
8
Who has ever seen anything as strange as this?
Who ever heard of such a thing?
Has a nation ever been born in a single day?
Has a country ever come forth in a mere moment?

*But by the time Jerusalem's birth pains begin,
her children will be born.*

In AD 70 the Romans attacked Jerusalem, and the Jews were scattered across the world. No Israel nation existed again until 1948. The land that was Israel was under the control of England. After World War ll and the Holocaust England saw fit to honor an agreement from 1917 called the Balfour agreement. This action therefore recognized Israel as the country it formerly was. This occurred in one day on May 14, 1948.

This prophecy in Isaiah was written in approximately 700 BC. Therefore 2600 years past before it was fulfilled in 1948. In history no nation has ever been destroyed and scattered and then returned to be a nation again!

Continuing in Isaiah is the prophecy of the Jews return to Israel:

Isaiah 43:5-6 (ESV)
5
*Fear not, for I am with you;
I will bring your offspring from the east,
and from the west I will gather you.*
6
*I will say to the north, Give up,
and to the south, Do not withhold;
bring my sons from afar
and my daughters from the end of the earth,*

Ezekiel 11:16-17 (ESV)
16 Therefore say, 'Thus says the Lord God: Though I removed them far off among the nations, and though I scattered them among the countries, yet I have been a sanctuary to them for a while in the countries where they have gone.' 17 Therefore say, 'Thus says the Lord God: I will gather you from the peoples and assemble you out of the countries where you have been scattered, and I will give you the land of Israel.'

In 1948 when Israel was reestablished as a nation there were approximately 600,000 Jews living there. The Jews have returned from afar and today about eight and a half million people live there.

In Matthew 24:14 Jesus said that the Gospel will be preached throughout the world.

Matthew 24:14 (ESV)
14 And this gospel of the kingdom will be proclaimed throughout the whole world as a testimony to all nations, and then the end will come.

Today there are missionaries in every country. The Bible has been translated in hundreds of languages and are continuing to add more. The message of Jesus is sent around the world by radio, TV, satellite, and the Internet. Our generation is literally on the verge of insuring the spreading the gospel to every last person on earth.

There will be in increase in knowledge and travel. Daniel 12:4 says:

Daniel 12:4 (NLT)
4 But you, Daniel, keep this prophecy a secret; seal up the book until the time of the end, when many will rush here and there, and knowledge will increase."

Today you can travel halfway across the world in a matter of hours when in the Biblical days it would take a number of hours to go twenty miles.

Today you can get all the knowledge you want or need by using the internet. News from across the globe can be read, seen, and heard in a matter of minutes.

Israel Surrounded by Enemies

Psalm 83:4 (ESV)
4
They say, "Come, let us wipe them out as a nation;
let the name of Israel be remembered no more!"

This verse is almost a perfect match for some of the things Iran has said. Israel is also hated by Syria, Libya, and Russia. Israel's Muslim neighbors claim the land of Israel for themselves, and they have no regard for the God of Israel.

The Rise of Global Government

The Bible provides evidence to enable us to draw the conclusion that a one world government and one world currency will exist under the rule of the Antichrist in the last days. You can see this drawn out in Revelation 13 and Daniel 7:16-24.

The antichrist will rule during the Tribulation for 7 years. During this time he will require that everyone be given a mark on their forehead or on the right hand. No one will be able to buy or sell anything without this mark (Revelation 13:16-17).

Revelation 13:16-17 (ESV)
16 *Also it causes all, both small and great, both rich and poor, both free and slave, to be marked on the right hand or the forehead, 17 so that no one can buy or sell unless he has the mark, that is, the name of the beast or the number of its name.*

Today, right now, you can see the move from global leaders pushing for a global, one world, government. This one world government has been endorsed by President's Obama and George H. W. Bush, but many others have voiced similar statements. Among them are Robert Kennedy, Bill Clinton, David Rockefeller, Winston Churchill, Franklin Roosevelt, and even Walter Cronkite (if any of you young people have ever heard of him).

The moves towards a one world government and one world currency are extremely evident in today's society. The push for open borders is for the goal of a one world government. The increasing responsibilities of the United Nations is a step towards a one world government. In fact that creating a New World Order is enshrined in the U.N. Charter. Globalists have already created a number of organizations geared towards various issues based on the worlds needs or desires. Among them:

The World Bank
The International Criminals Court
The International Monetary Fund
The Bank for International Settlements
The World Trade Organization
The World Health Organization
The World Court

The Rise of Global Currency

Signs are also strong in the move towards a one world currency. There are strong trends throughout the world of going to a cashless society. Sweden is approximately 95% cashless at this time. India has plans of going cashless. Here, in the USA, Visa has a program in place trying to get restaurants to stop using cash. Once cash goes away it will be quite easy for the antichrist to institute his plan of no buying or selling without his mark. Technological advances will make this extremely easy to enforce.

Rise of the Gog of Magog Alliance

In the book of Ezekiel, chapter 38, you will read about what is called the War of Gog and Magog.

Ezekiel 38:1-6 (ESV)

1 *The word of the Lord came to me:* **2** *"Son of man, set your face toward Gog, of the land of Magog, the chief prince of Meshech and Tubal, and prophesy against him* **3** *and say, Thus says the Lord God: Behold, I am against you, O Gog, chief prince of Meshech and Tubal.* **4** *And I will turn you about and put hooks into your jaws, and I will bring you out, and all your army, horses and horsemen, all of them clothed in full armor, a great host, all of them with buckler and shield, wielding swords.* **5** *Persia, Cush, and Put are with them, all of them with shield and helmet;* **6** *Gomer and all his hordes; Beth-togarmah from the uttermost parts of the north with all his hordes—many peoples are with you.*

These first six verses of chapter 38 identify the participants of the was that will attack Israel.

Ezekiel 38:17-23 (ESV)

17 *"Thus says the Lord God: Are you he of whom I spoke in former days by my servants the prophets of Israel, who in those days prophesied for years that I would bring you against them?* **18** *But on that day, the day that Gog shall come against the land of Israel, declares the Lord God, my wrath will be roused in my anger.* **19** *For in my jealousy and in my blazing wrath I declare, On that day there shall be a great earthquake in the land of Israel.* **20** *The fish of the sea and the birds of the heavens and the beasts of the field and all creeping things that creep on the ground, and all the people who are on the face of the earth, shall quake at my presence. And the mountains shall be thrown down, and the cliffs shall fall, and every wall shall tumble to the ground.* **21** *I will summon a sword against Gog on all my mountains, declares the Lord God. Every man's sword will be* *against his brother. **22** With pestilence and bloodshed I will enter into judgment with him, and I will rain upon him and his hordes and the many peoples who are with him torrential rains and hailstones, fire and sulfur. **23** So I will show my greatness and my holiness and make myself known in the eyes of many nations. Then they will know that I am the Lord.*

Verses 17-23 describes what happens to the armies that plan on attacking Israel. Note the supernatural happenings caused by God that takes place against these attacking forces. Gods says:

On that day there will be a great earthquake. Mountains will be thrown down, cliffs shall fall, every wall will tumble to the ground. Every man will turn again his brother. Torrential rains and hailstorms, fire and sulfur will all effect the enemy. And then Israel and the world will know who God is.

Many pastors believe this war will take place in the Tribulation, but it is possible that it could occur before then. I put this in my book for one reason. Look at the nations who bound together to attack Israel. Magog, Rosh, Persia, Cush, Put, Gomer, Meshech, Tubal, and Beth-togarmah. This was the name by which these nations were known when Ezekiel wrote his book. Today these nations are known as:

Magog, Rosh = Russia and the former Soviet republics

Persia = Iran

Cush = Sudan, Ethiopia, and Possibly Eritrea

Put = Libya, Algeria, and Tunisa

Gomer, Meshech, and Tubal = Turkey (and possibly Germany and Austria)

Beth-togarmah = Turkey, Armenia, Turkish-speaking people of Asia Minor & Central Asia

Look at this list and see who the major players are today: Russia, Iran, Libya, and Turkey. Iran and Russia have formed a military alliance. Never before in history have they been allies. Turkey has turned its back on Israel and is now supporting Iran and Russia. One of the main things in common with these countries will be its Muslim ties. Iran and Turkey will be united by this. Russia's interest will primarily be money because Israel has become, and will continue to be, a very wealthy country.

So this war is a part of my writings on prophecy for you to keep your eye on. This war will happen, and the world will take note.

The Jewish Temple

In AD 70 when the Romans attacked Jerusalem as Jesus prophesied in Matthew 24:1-2 the Jewish Temple was destroyed with no stone standing just as Jesus said. It has never been rebuilt. But that has not stopped the planning to build a new temple. The temple will exist in the Tribulation because we read in Daniel 9:27 and Matthew 24:15 that the antichrist will create an abomination of desolation by standing in the third temple proclaiming to be God.

Daniel 9:27 (ESV)
27 And he shall make a strong covenant with many for one week, and for half of the week he shall put an end to sacrifice and offering. And on the wing of abominations shall come one who makes desolate, until the decreed end is poured out on the desolator."

Matthew 24:15 (ESV) The Abomination of Desolation
15 "So when you see the abomination of desolation spoken of by the prophet Daniel, standing in the holy place (let the reader understand),

2 Thessalonians 2:4 (ESV)
4 who opposes and exalts himself against every so-called god or object of worship, so that he takes his seat in the temple of God, proclaiming himself to be God.

Now in order for this to happen the Temple will have to be rebuilt. I bring this up to tell you that plans are underway to build the third temple. The Temple Institute has been working tirelessly for the past

30-plus years to recreate all the items needed for the rebuilt Jewish Temple. Most, if not all, these items have been reproduced, the temple has been designed, and even a red heifer has been produced to begin the offerings. You can read about these plans at TheTempleInstitute.Org.

The Exponential Curve

One view I've seen expressed is called the the "exponential curve".

Mark 13:29-30 (ESV)
29 *So also, when you see these things taking place, you know that he is near, at the very gates.* **30** *Truly, I say to you, this generation will not pass away until all these things take place.*

Jesus says here in Mark "when you see these things taking place you know that he is near".

Here is what I mean about the exponential curve. Israel is back in the land, the Jews have returned to Israel, the gospel is being preached throughout the world, knowledge and travel are greatly increased, Israel is surrounded by enemies, plans are underway for a one world government, a one world currency, and a new Temple .

Now that we have seen these prophecies fulfilled, or being fulfilled, let me explain the exponential curve. From the ancient times look at how fast we now advance and things now change. The Wright brothers engineered flying planes around 1903. In 1969 we had men land on the moon. In just 66 years we had gone from not being able to fly at all to landing on the moon. Look at computers. In the early days of computers it would take a whole room to be able to be able to fit a computer in it. Today you can take what was in that entire room and more and fit it into an iPhone. Technology is moving at an alarming rate. Things are on an uphill swing constantly.

So if all of these things are falling into place, and quickly, can you see Jesus returning soon? As Jesus said in Mark 13:29 "when you see these things taking place you know that he is near". And in verse 30

He says, " this generation will not pass away until all these things take place." Can you see why many pastors believe the Rapture is close?

Some of the prophecies will be fulfilled in the Tribulation. But the true Christians following Christ now will not be here because the Rapture will take them before the Tribulation begin.

EPILOGUE

1 John 2:15-17 (ESV)
15 Do not love the world or the things in the world. If anyone loves the world, the love of the Father is not in him. 16 For all that is in the world—the desires of the flesh and the desires of the eyes and pride of life—is not from the Father but is from the world. 17 And the world is passing away along with its desires, but whoever does the will of God abides forever.

A True Christian is NOTW. **Not Of This World!**

Jesus knows what trouble we would have living on this earth in this world with its evil culture. Jesus prays for us, those left behind on this earth, in John chapter 17. The entire chapter is Jesus' prayer and, we learn that the world is a tremendous battleground where the forces under Satan's power and those under God's authority are at war. Satan and his forces are motivated by bitter hatred for Christ and his followers. Jesus prayed for his disciples, including those of us who follow him today. He prayed that God would keep his chosen believers safe from Satan's power, setting them apart and making them pure and holy, uniting them through his truth.

My inspiration for writing this book came from two millennials misunderstanding of the importance of Jesus Christ in our lives, and the influence He should have on us in the culture in which we live. The world, our culture, has drastically changed from the Baby Boomer generation to the current generations.

In the Baby Boomer generation:
- Teens getting pregnant was an embarrassment

- Abortion was illegal
- Couples living together were rare
- Adultery was sinful
- Possession of marijuana was a felony
- If a student could not learn he failed the class or grade
- Trophies were only given to winners in youth sports
- Prayer was in schools
- Our country was loved
- Homosexuals were in the closet
- Everyone was not a Christian, **but Christianity was respected**

Now, today, in regards to the list above everything has changed. Its nothing for a teen to get pregnant, and if they don't want the child they can abort it. Couples live together all the time, and they don't see anything wrong with it. Web sites exist to provide cover for people who want to cheat on their spouse, many states have legalized the use of marijuana, students are sent to higher grades without learning, trophies are given to all who participate in sports, and the homosexual agenda is the biggest threat to Christianity because of their persistent attacks on anyone or anything that doesn't bless their sinful life.

Being a Christian is turning away from all types of these activities and sins. **A Christian cannot accept them, condone them, or make excuses for them**.

Romans 12:2 (ESV)
2 Do not be conformed to this world, but be transformed by the renewal of your mind, that by testing you may discern what is the will of God, what is good and acceptable and perfect.

The Kingdom of God is not for people who want Jesus without any change in their lives. It is only for those who "seek it with all their hearts". The Kingdom of God is for those who recognize the sin in their lives and want to rid themselves of that sin. The Kingdom of

God is for those believers who feel guilty when they do sin and want forgiveness for that sin.

Receiving Christ does not mean we can merely add Jesus to the refuse of our lives.

Salvation is a total transformation:

2 Corinthians 5:17 (ESV)
17 *Therefore, if anyone is in Christ, he is a new creation. The old has passed away; behold, the new has come.*

Old things pass away. Sin and selfishness and worldly pleasure are replaced by new things. This is the whole point of salvation: it produces a changed life. Jesus does not want casual followers, but people who give their lives to Him. True believers will persevere. They will live their lives 100% for Him. Professing Christians who turn against the Lord only prove that they were never truly saved.

The disciple Judas and his life of deceit is a warning to those who casually profess their faith in Jesus. Judas was never really saved.

John 12:6 (ESV)
6 *He (Judas) said this, not because he cared about the poor, but because he was a thief, and having charge of the moneybag he used to help himself to what was put into it.*

John 13:10-11 (ESV)
10 *Jesus said to him, "The one who has bathed does not need to wash, except for his feet, but is completely clean. And you are clean, but not every one of you."* **11** *For he knew who was to betray him; that was why he said, "Not all of you are clean."*

Judas was lost forever. That frightening potential exists for every person who comes to Christ without a committed heart.

Many who think they are saved will be shocked to discover in the final judgment that heaven is not their destiny.

Matthew 7:21-23 (ESV)
21 *"Not everyone who says to me, 'Lord, Lord,' will enter the kingdom of heaven, but the one who does the will of my Father who is in heaven.* **22** *On that day many will say to me, 'Lord, Lord, did we not prophesy in your name, and cast out demons in your name, and do many mighty works in your name?'* **23** *And then will I declare to them, 'I never knew you; depart from me, you workers of lawlessness.'*

Look at the phrase in verse 21, identifying the kind of person who will inhabit heaven. It is **"the one who does the will of My Father."** It is not the one who says he knows Jesus or who believes certain facts about Him. It is the one who does the Father's will. And look at verse 23, **"depart from me"**.

Scripture encourages spiritual self-examination. In 2 Corinthians 13:5 Paul wrote:

2 Corinthians 13:5 (ESV)
Examine yourselves, to see whether you are in the faith. Test yourselves. Or do you not realize this about yourselves, that Jesus Christ is in you?—unless indeed you fail to meet the test!

We are called to examine and test ourselves to see if we really are Christians. Paul urges us to give ourselves spiritual checkups. We should look for a growing awareness of Christ's presence and power in our lives. Only then will we know if we are true Christians or merely impostors. **If we're not actively seeking to grow closer to God, we are drawing farther away from him.**

The heart of true Christian discipleship is a commitment to be like Jesus Christ. That means both acting as He did and being willing to accept the same treatment. It means facing a world that is hostile to

Him and doing it fearlessly. It means confessing before others that Jesus is Lord and being confident that He will also speak on our behalf before the Father.

The will of God for us on this earth is for a lifetime:
1. Pursue the will of God above all else.
2. Proving the will of God.
3. Practicing the will of God.

We are God's masterpiece. He has a plan for everyday of your life. It is never too late to become the person God made you to be.

Ephesians 2:10 (NLT)
For we are God's masterpiece. He has created us anew in Christ Jesus, so we can do the good things he planned for us long ago.

Ask yourself this question. **Where would I be without the cross?**

Definitions:
Sacred - devoted or dedicated to a deity (God) or to some religious purpose
Secular - of or relating to worldly things or to things that are not regarded as religious, spiritual, or sacred
Now ask yourself this question. How much of your daily time do you spend on sacred things? Five percent, maybe 10 or 40, as much as 50%.
To address this question I would first go to God's Word:

1 Corinthians 10:31 (ESV)
So, whether you eat or drink, or whatever you do, do all to the glory of God.

This verse tells us that every action we take must be motivated by God's loves so that all we do will be for His glory. Every breath we take, every thought we have, every decision we make we should consider how this fits into God's plan. Everything on this earth is connected to God! Will He approve? Will He condone? Will it give God glory?

So the right thing we do is for us to be sacred 100% if the time. So, if your are not giving God 100% of you, why not?

Let's make our lives count. ***Give God an undivided life.***

1. Acknowledge God continually   Psalms 139:1-7
2. Trust in God completely   Proverbs 3:5-6
3. Represent God daily   2 Corinthians 5:20

Psalm 139:1-7 (ESV)

1 O Lord, you have searched me and known me!
2 You know when I sit down and when I rise up;
you discern my thoughts from afar.
3 You search out my path and my lying down
and are acquainted with all my ways.
4 Even before a word is on my tongue,
behold, O Lord, you know it altogether.
5 You hem me in, behind and before,
and lay your hand upon me.
6 Such knowledge is too wonderful for me;
it is high; I cannot attain it.
7 Where shall I go from your Spirit?
Or where shall I flee from your presence?

Proverbs 3:5-6 (ESV)

5 Trust in the Lord with all your heart,
and do not lean on your own understanding.
6 In all your ways acknowledge him,
and he will make straight your paths.

2 Corinthians 5:20 (ESV)
20 *Therefore, we are ambassadors for Christ, God making his appeal through us. We implore you on behalf of Christ, be reconciled to God.*

The world doesn't revolve around you or me. It revolves around God. Our primary purpose for existence is to glorify the Lord our God.

This is the way John the Baptist said it about Jesus:

John 3:30 (ESV)
He must increase, but I must decrease."

God's priority is that He receive all the honor and glory. God doesn't do everything so His glory will be revealed for His own good. God wants His glory revealed in everything that happens **for *our good* so we can witness His glory. God wants us to see His glory so we can reflect it to the rest of the world.**

1 Chronicles 16:24 (ESV)
Declare his glory among the nations, his marvelous works among all the peoples!

Everything you do is for God's glory!
Your success if for God's glory
Your body is is to be used for God's glory
Your struggles are to be used for God's glory

Any success you have has been given to you by God to bring Him glory. You are to use your body to God's glory with sexual purity and healthy eating habits etc. Your body is God's temple. When people see you put God first in your struggles He will be glorified.

Here are some important questions to ask yourself as you go about your day living 100% for God:
  * Is my behavior constructive to other people?

* Am I looking out for self or the other person?
* Does my behavior point others to God?
* Does my behavior cause others to stumble?
* Do our words point others to Christ.
* Do our actions point others to Christ.
* Does our attitude point others to Christ.

Our mission, and God's desire, is that He be honored in every area of our lives. We do not exclude anything, even the things we eat or drink as explained in 1 Corinthians 10:31.

When we put Christ first we should be willing to bring all things before Him. Consideration for Him should affect ALL decisions we make.

Live every second, minute, hour, day, month, lifetime 100% for Jesus Christ. For His glory!

I want to thank you very much for reading my book. I pray that you have learned something that will be helpful to you or something you can pass along to others to help them develop a love, following, and devotion to Jesus Christ.

My plea, and my prayer, to you is that if you object or disagree with something I said please don't just ignore it. Research what I have written, determine for yourself if what I have written is true or false. Do all you can to determine what the Word of God says!

If you have any questions or comments feel free to email me at:
50.STARS@REAGAN.COM

God bless you all!

ADDENDUM

The prophet Jeremiah warned Israel and Jerusalem for 40 years that if they did not turn from their idols and evil ways that they would be overtaken by another ruler. In 586 B.C. his prophesy came true. Babylonian King Nebuchadnezzer's army invaded Israel and destroyed Jerusalem and the Temple.

Jeremiah 52:12-14 (NLT)
12 On August 17 of that year, which was the nineteenth year of King Nebuchadnezzar's reign, Nebuzaradan, the captain of the guard and an official of the Babylonian king, arrived in Jerusalem. 13 He burned down the Temple of the Lord, the royal palace, and all the houses of Jerusalem. He destroyed all the important buildings in the city. 14 Then he supervised the entire Babylonian army as they tore down the walls of Jerusalem on every side.

Jeremiah's warnings, sent directly from God, had gone unheeded. Jeremiah is known as the "Weeping Prophet" because his love for his homeland left him in tears because they did not follow the Words of God and ended up destroyed. In the book of Lamentations Jeremiah recounts all of the hurt and sorrow that Jerusalem experienced after King Nebuchadnezzar's invasion.

Lamentations 1:9 NLT
She defiled herself with immorality and gave no thought to her future. Now she lies in the gutter with no one to lift her out. " LORD, see my misery," she cries. " The enemy has triumphed."

The warning was loud and clear: If Judah played with fire, its people would get burned. Jerusalem foolishly took a chance and lost, refusing to believe that immoral living brings God's punishment. **The ultimate consequence of sin is punishment!**

Folks this is where America is right now, and frankly the whole world is too. Like Jeremiah I grieve for our great country. Our country has ignored the Word of God. He has not only been pushed aside, our country has tried to eliminate Him altogether. God's Word is full of warnings to sinners to turn from their evil ways. We can choose to ignore God's warnings, but as surely as judgment came upon Jerusalem, so will it come upon those who defy God.

Obedience is the only sure sign of your love for God.

www.ingramcontent.com/pod-product-compliance
Lightning Source LLC
Chambersburg PA
CBHW071515040426
42444CB00008B/1652